STORYTELLER

"Talent and luck are always critical factors, but common sense and realistic expectations also go a long way toward turning would-be writers into published authors. Few of us have enjoyed Carlton Stowers's much-deserved level of success—bestsellers, major awards, movie deals—but your chance will greatly increase if you read and learn from Storyteller. It offers advice from an acknowledged master, and I wish to hell it had been available when I was trying to get started."

— JEFF GUINN, *New York Times* bestselling author
of both fiction and nonfiction and member of the
Texas Literary Hall of Fame

"This is an excellent book for aspiring writers. Carlton Stowers, a masterful storyteller and prolific author, shares his practical wisdom and expertise about what it takes to be successful."

— GLENN DROMGOOLE, author of more than thirty books
and Texas Literary Hall of Fame member

"Whatever it is that makes a writer a writer, Carlton Stowers has it. And to prove it, he has written the best book on writing I have ever read."

— DAVID MCHAM, honored college journalism professor
(from the foreword)

STORYTELLER

Helpful Hints and Tall Tales
from the Writing Life

Carlton Stowers

★ TEXAS WRITERS SERIES

Fort Worth, Texas

Library of Congress Cataloging-in-Publication Data

Names: Stowers, Carlton, author.
Title: Storyteller : a handbook of helpful hints and tall tales from the
    writing life / Carlton Stowers.
Description: Fort Worth : TCU Press, [2025] | "It is a book about the
    crapshoot craft of writing as I have experienced it, a confession as
    much as a tutorial."--ECIP page 10. | Includes bibliographical
    references. | Summary: "During his lengthy writing career, Carlton
    Stowers has had his highs and lows, all the while learning more and more
    about his chosen craft. In STORYTELLER, he chronicles the pitfalls and
    prat falls, suggests how best to pitch a book or article to editors, the
    do's and don'ts of research and interviewing. While spinning a humorous
    story or two along the way, the author touches on the entire spectrum of
    writing for a living, producing what iconic university journalism
    professor David McHam calls "the best book on writing I've ever
    read.""-- Provided by publisher.
Identifiers: LCCN 2024045168 (print) | LCCN 2024045169 (ebook) | ISBN
    9780875659046 (paperback) | ISBN 9780875659190 (ebook)
Subjects: LCSH: Stowers, Carlton. | Authors, American--Texas--Biography. |
    Journalists--Texas--Biography. | Self-employed--Texas--Biography. |
    Freelance journalism--Vocational guidance. | Feature writing--Vocational
    guidance. | Authorship--Marketing--Vocational guidance. | LCGFT:
    Autobiographies. | Creative nonfiction. | Handbooks and manuals.
Classification: LCC PS3619.T6995 Z46 2025 (print) | LCC PS3619.T6995
    (ebook) | DDC 814/.6--dc23/eng/20240927
LC record available at https://lccn.loc.gov/2024045168
LC ebook record available at https://lccn.loc.gov/2024045169

TCU Box 298300
Fort Worth, Texas 76129
www.tcupress.com

Design by Bill Brammer

Dedication

For my pal Max, who has never read a word I've written,
yet sits dutifully at my feet, keeping watch.

... and, of course, to Pat,
who long encouraged this project.

"Writing comes from reading, and reading is the finest teacher of how to write."

ANNIE PROULX

"Read, read, read. Read everything—trash, classics, good and bad, and see how they do it. Just like a carpenter who works as an apprentice and studies the master. Read. You'll absorb it. Then write."

WILLIAM FAULKNER

TABLE OF CONTENTS

Foreword

———

This is a tale about one of Texas's best storytellers.

It begins in little Ballinger in West Texas in the 1950s when he showed such athletic promise that it led to him and his family making a move to Abilene before he entered high school. There, he participated in an Abilene High football program that established a national record forty-nine consecutive victories. He excelled in track, serving as cocaptain of the 1960 team that won the state championship.

He received a scholarship to the University of Texas, where, in addition to leading off a nationally ranked 440-yard relay, he found his calling. He began writing for the campus newspaper.

Years later, he covered the Dallas Cowboys for the *Dallas Morning News* before becoming a full-time freelance writer. He has written a series of true crime books, twice winning the Edgar Allan Poe Award for the year's best. To date, he has written fifty nonfiction and fiction books as well as articles for a variety of national and regional publications. My favorite of his books is *Where Dreams Die Hard*, a heartwarming story set in the tiny town of Penelope, Texas.

Whatever it is that makes a writer a writer, Carlton Stowers has it. And to prove it, he has written the best book on writing I have ever read.

—DAVID MCHAM

David McHam's distinguished career as a collegiate journalism professor included tenures at Baylor, Southern Methodist, the University of Texas–Arlington, and the University of Houston before his retirement. In 1994, the Society of Professional Journalism named him the nation's outstanding journalism teacher.

What This Is Not

ON THE PAGES TO FOLLOW there are no hidden clues to attaining great wealth or any secret road map to the *New York Times* bestseller list. Rest assured that no false promises will be made. This is neither a primer of hard-and-fast rules nor a do-it-my-way-or-the-highway exercise. It is but a grab bag of well-intended suggestions from one who has, during a career that began long before cell phones, the internet, YouTube, or even the magic of word processors, made myriad mistakes he hopes to steer you from.

It is a book about the crapshoot craft of writing as I have experienced it, a confession as much as a tutorial. As to my credentials, I have no bulging account in the Caymans, no on-call publicist, not even a website to call my own. I am simply one of the millions who tries daily to write something that will pass an editor's muster, interest the reader, and result in an income adequate to keep the lights on and groceries in the fridge. High finance and I have never met.

And, so long as we're being completely honest, I'm aware that there have already been too many books on this subject, some authored by those with more impressive academic credentials and sales records. All I'm offering is my two cents' worth. And, as it has been proven, there is always room for one more revisit to a subject. My all-time favorite book title, after all, is *The 100 Best Books on Abraham Lincoln*. I kid you not.

I began my writing career in the newspaper business, a former high school and college jock who once viewed sports writing as journalism's highest calling. It was fun and, for a time, fulfilling. The pay wasn't bad and, hey, I got into the games free.

There came a time, however, when I felt a growing urge to broaden my professional horizons. I began writing for magazines, some top of the line, like *Sports Illustrated, Good Housekeeping, Parade*, and many others you've never heard of. A favorite I recall in the latter category was a story I did on a gang of old-time bank robbing brothers for a little publication called *Grain Producers News*. I think it mailed me a check for twenty-five dollars.

Freelance Writing

————

I AM WHAT IS KNOWN in journalism circles as a freelance writer, which loosely translates to being self-unemployed and willing to accept any assignment offered, even if it requires typing with one hand while holding one's nose with the other.

One of the most valuable lesson any freelancer will learn—most often the hard way—is this: never say no to *Grain Producer News* while waiting for *Good Housekeeping* to call and offer the big bucks. There is no assignment too insignificant to ignore. While waiting for the windfall check from *Vanity Fair*, go ahead and deposit those received from the needy tabloids, trade journals, and monthlies spouting the mantra of the local chambers of commerce.

Most often, I've been smiled on. Over the years, the worthwhile projects have far outweighed those that made me want to consider selling used cars or term life for a living. To this day, my two thousand ground-out words on "A Day in the Life of a Meter Reader," a profile of an orthodontist who came up with the strange notion of attaching braces into the mouths of dolls brought to his office by his young female patients, and coverage of my first soccer game remain deadlocked at the absolute bottom of a sizable pile.

I should also include a last-minute assignment to cover a stump speech of a particular presidential candidate for *Time* magazine. Blissfully ignorant of and totally disinterested in politics, I accepted, then had to ask my savvy wife what party the speaker was affiliated with. Accepting the assignment probably wasn't among my smartest moves.

Having already told you to accept any job that's legal, be aware that the darkest trap a beginning writer can fall into is attempting to write on subjects about which he has absolutely no interest or expertise.

Trust me, it will show in your finished product, and it won't be pretty. The time-tested axiom—write what you know—remains one to live by.

And, if you're fortunate enough to find a small selection of publications who like your work, keep them happy. Give them your best reporting, meet their deadlines, and you can bet they'll be back in touch or will listen to your next idea.

Back in my scatter shooting days, I developed a good relationship with the editor at the weekly Sunday magazine published by the *Dallas Morning News*, a newspaper I would later work for. Though city born and raised, the editor shared my fondness for under-the-radar stories in out of the way places and accepted most of my ideas. He once confided to me that during a year's time, I produced more published pieces than any of the three salaried members of his staff.

If one doesn't mind jumping and running, there are the weekly national publications that dip from a bottomless editorial bucket. I'll have more to say later about a teacher in a one-room school in the middle of nowhere who I profiled for *People* magazine. That story, happened on by sheer accident, launched a decades-long relationship with the publication. In time, I became one of its regular correspondents and got first-name familiar with the Dallas Fort Worth airport.

The assignments ranged from stories I suggested to ones they came up with. Some were even history-in-the-making. I joined a team of reporters on-site at the infamous Oklahoma City federal building bombing and spent over a month in Waco during the ugly Branch Davidian standoff. An editor dispatched me to cover the aftermath of the Pearl, Mississippi, school shooting. I wrote about a small-town Sunday School teacher who killed his elderly female companion and hid her body in a freezer for months before his crime was discovered, and I contributed to a cover story on the death of Major League Baseball icon Mickey Mantle.

Every new assignment was a surprise.

Writing for news magazines is a strange breed of freelance journalism. Here's how it works:

When you're assigned a story, it is your reporting they want. They require a comprehensive "file," as they call it, which includes every detail of every person you interview, including their birthdate. Though the file you send may closely resemble a traditional magazine piece, it will be turned over to an in-house writer who will melt it down to the short story style of the publication. His or her byline will appear at the top of the piece while at the end there will be a "Reporting by . . ." line.

The same practice was applied by *Time* on the occasional pieces I reported for it.

Writing for such publications, then, is a good news–bummer situation, particularly if the subject is your idea and the reporting done exclusively by you. We all enjoy our own bylines. But the assignments were most often quick turnaround and fast pay. And, after you play little mind games with them for a bit, you just might get lucky now and then and see that the dandy lede you wrote for your file made it onto the pages of the magazine.

Also, be aware that lead time is a concept foreign to those in News Magazine Central. In my mind, I always saw the assignment editors frantically rushing from a meeting room to call. Like those great old movie trial scenes where the guilty verdict is announced and reporters elbow and collide as they race to the lobby phone bank. Even the most routine story was a three-alarm emergency. As a friend once explained to me in this ego-deflating observation: Pal, they need your little stories to keep all those ads from bumping into each other.

One morning, as I was dutifully mowing the yard, I received an urgent call assigning me to do quick interviews with a half dozen freed Iran hostages who were flying home to Midland, Texas. They had a brief layover and carrier change to Southwest Airlines in Dallas, and I needed to get there and talk with each of them ASAP.

Though I rushed to the airport, my subjects were about to board for the final leg of their freedom by the time I arrived. I quickly bought a ticket and joined them. Before we landed, I had managed to get midair quotes from everyone. I viewed the terminal homecoming celebration, then got an immediate return flight home. My wife, who had been busy running errands that day, never knew I was gone.

Over the years as I continued to do work for *People*, I came to a realization that squared me with any ownership concerns I felt for the stories I submitted to them. Everyone who writes wants to reach as many readers as possible. There were numerous times when I'd come across an idea that I was certain I could sell to a smaller regional publication after writing it the way I felt it should be written. But, when I would remind myself of the millions of readers *People* had, the choice got easier. Bottom line: a storyteller likes as big an audience as possible.

And believe me, announcing yourself as a reporter on assignment from *People* magazine opens a lot of doors.

Too, there is the matter of immediacy that many story ideas demand. The problem is easier dealt with by a weekly publication than one that comes out monthly. I knew, for instance, that word would quickly spread about a strange fella named Bernie Teide who had murdered his lady friend, then hid her body under the frozen vegetables in the freezer.

In a brief phone call, *People* said, yes, do it. And hurry.

Readers coast-to-coast had read my story long before *Texas Monthly*'s talented Skip Hollandsworth even did his first interview. Those of us raised in the newspaper business still get a kick out of beating the other guy to a scoop whenever possible.

In all fairness, however, I must point out that Skip's belated take was far more detailed, a great read, and evolved into the movie *Bernie*, for which he was even invited to cowrite the screenplay. You win some, lose some, and move on.

Before leaving this subject, I should point out that the tabloids, those grocery checkout line publications that everyone hides in the bottom of their bag, operate in much the same manner as the news magazines. They can't fill all their pages with the Kardashians and miracle cures every week, so they, too, are looking for interesting nonscandalous stories. They like the small town, offbeat yarns as much as the rural-targeted *Grit* once did. (The introductory story I did for the *National Enquirer* was on the first hotel Conrad Hilton owned, a two-story brick structure in the little oil boom town of Cisco, Texas.)

Like *People* and *Time*, the tabloids also ask that you submit a file. The finished product will carry the byline of one of their staff writers.

Truth is, some image-conscious freelancers might be relieved that their name won't appear in the publications. It never made me much different so long as the story was accurate, offended no one, and the check didn't bounce. Neither did a cover story I once did for small wages for *Front Page Detective*, another publication that's never earned a nod from the Pulitzer committee. I do recall its editor sending me a nice hand-written note in which he "wished he had other contributors who could write as well."

What it boils down to is everyone must start somewhere. For years, acclaimed true crime author Ann Rule honed her craft by writing almost exclusively for the pulpy detective magazines under the pen name Andy Stack. Along the way she polished her considerable skills and became a constant bestseller in hardback.

In time came my step up to book writing. Over the years, I would write biographies, ghost autobiographies, do corporate histories, and compose books on horrifying crimes, small town life, and sports—in addition to writing a half dozen paperback western novels. My dad always referred to the latter as "shoot 'em ups," but he'd have been prouder of those than any cover story for *TV Guide*, interviews with Super Bowl MVP Roger Staubach, or the life story I helped movie icons Roy Rogers and Dale Evans write.

I point such matters out not as any apology for my resume being all over the map but to suggest I just might have something worthwhile to pass along on a variety of topics—from reporting to column writing, profiles to investigative journalism, and how to write books on Olympic champions, stealthy private eyes, and a death row chaplain. Hey, I've even had a poem or two make it into print.

I've always wanted to tag along the backroads and write about a Bible-thumping tent revival troupe, but it's just never worked out. It's still on the bucket list, however.

It is all writing, putting words into meaningful sentences that connect the reader to the subject. It boils down to storytelling that is educating, entertaining, and well written.

Days of an Ink-Stained Wretch

———

I BEGGED A ONE-DAY DELAY of my first wedding so I could cover a high school football game.

That right there should tell you a couple of things. First, I was deadly determined to earn my place in the newspaper business. Second, there wasn't much hope for a blissful union. Right on both counts. The feature I wrote ultimately received a one hundred dollar award and certificate from the William Randolph Hearst Foundation. The marriage failed.

My loftiest goal upon arriving on the University of Texas campus early in the 1960s was to earn a letter as a productive member of the Longhorns track team. The first in my family to attend college, I had no idea about a major. Only when, early in my sophomore year, I stumbled into the little editorial office of the campus newspaper, the *Daily Texan*, did a brainstorm occur. A journalism degree required far less math, foreign language, or brain-numbing science labs. How difficult could it be?

Since the starting salary for a *Daily Texan* sportswriter was nothing, all applicants were given equal consideration. I was promised a tryout and assigned to cover the upcoming the Southwest Conference cross-country championships. I wrote the hell out of the story, turning in several pages of high-drama prose.

When I viewed the next day's edition, I found that the editor, a rather overbearing senior, had cut it to two paragraphs, neither which resembled anything I'd initially written.

In time, however, I began to get the hang of it. I wrote headlines, fetched late-night hamburgers for my superiors, learned about page layouts, and enrolled in Feature Writing 101. Even wrote a story or two proudly accompanied by a byline. Mostly, I hung around the others on the staff, listening and learning. And I pored over the sports pages of the myriad newspapers that arrived daily in the journalism building library. I also talked my way into a twice-weekly nighttime job answering phones for the *Austin American-Statesman* sports department.

It all melded into a giant-sized classroom, and I soon realized that just beyond it was an exciting world I badly wanted to be part of.

A year or so after my cross-country reporting debacle, I began climbing the ladder. I wrote something almost daily and even occasionally did a column. The most exciting of times were those football Saturdays when I sat in the same Memorial Stadium press box with the pros, big name sports journalists from all over the state. Occasionally, there would even be writers visiting from the *New York Times* or *Sports Illustrated*. To me, the company I found myself in was almost as exciting as the game we were watching. I couldn't wait to put higher learning behind and get out into the real world.

That I did late in my junior year. After long consideration, I sent out letters to alert several midsized papers that I was looking for a full-time job. When the sports editor of the *Abilene Reporter-News* responded with an offer, I thanked my understanding coach, a couple of favorite professors, withdrew from college, and was off to become part of the American workforce. I would be earning a handsome seventy-five dollars per week.

This is where I'm supposed to deliver my Stay in School message and pass along my deep regrets for not having earned a degree. Since I earlier promised to stick to the truth, I'll spare you. A diploma may be essential, even required, if you plan to one day be a healer, scientist, teacher, or high-paid barrister, but there are ways to learn to write that don't involve sky high student loans or endlessly sitting in a classroom.

It begins with reading. And more reading. Newspapers, magazines, books of fiction and nonfiction, the backside of cereal boxes. Okay, I'm kidding about the latter, but if you find reading boring and a waste of time, you'll never be a writer.

The best instruction for learning the craft that I've ever heard came from my old friend Giles Tippette, a successful author/journalist who I'll mention again later. During one of his numerous midlife crises, he decided to become a novelist. He asked around and concluded that *Adventures of Huckleberry Finn* was considered by many to be the closest we have to the Great American Novel.

Giles found a copy and read it—over and over and over. First, he simply read to enjoy Mark Twain's delightful story. Then, he reread to determine how the story was structured. Again, to learn things like how the characters' descriptions and their dialogue were used as the book's building blocks. Repeatedly, Giles said, he dissected the elements, major and minor, the author had used, peeling meat from the narrative bone until he could finally view the skeleton.

He went on to a long and distinguished career as a novelist and magazine writer. A theatrical movie based on one of his novels became a successful movie, *The Bank Robber*, starring Lee Marvin.

A. W. Gray, another pal, learned much the same way. With time on his hands while serving a prison sentence for some kind of dodgy insurance thing, he was reading an Elmore Leonard paperback when he decided maybe he, too, could be a mystery writer. He wore the paperback out, reading and rereading. Learning.

He located an aging typewriter in the prison library and began to write in the evenings. Finding that the old upright was without a return spool, he offered an old convicted burglar named Merkel a nightly pint of vanilla ice cream from the commissary to stand nearby and pull the worn ribbon through as he typed.

He sold his first novel, *Bino*, before his release.

Gray once asked Merkel how he got his name. "My mama had a lot of kids," his typewriter assistant explained. "When I came along, she called me her 'merkel baby.'"

I later used both anecdotes in pieces I would write—one in an introduction for a book collection of Tippette's magazine journalism and the other in a profile I wrote on Gray. (Hey, if you can't occasionally write about your friends . . .)

To this day, I view their approaches to learning to write light-years better than classroom lectures.

I recall one angry-at-the-world college professor who based a sizable percentage of her students' final grade on articles they had published in the campus daily. I felt home free—until midterm when she casually announced, for no good reason, she would not consider any sports stories in her final grading process. I left a note on her door to let her know I was dropping the course.

But, enough about college days and old friends.

I'm not sure the following pages I'd planned to devote to my days in the newspaper business are any longer relevant. With daily journalism on life support, papers downsizing or just giving up the ghost, staffs dwindling, and disappearing readers insisting that fair and balanced reporting is dead as a dinosaur, you might consider skipping ahead to a more worthwhile subject.

I say this not in jest but with great despair. For the aspiring writer, no better training ground has been invented than the newsroom, be it in a country weekly or metropolitan daily. Covering city council meetings, reporting from the cop shop, pounding an assigned beat, and chronicling the ups and downs of the local economy once provided the aspiring young writer an invaluable learning experience. Remember, even Ernest Hemingway was a war correspondent long before he became a household literary name. Before he evolved into an icon, he was learning about deadlines, educating his readers with short yet descriptive sentences, and building the self-discipline that is one of a writer's essential tools.

Had I not experienced the advantages of that training ground, I might be trying to convince you to purchase a one-owner used car or offering you a sale-priced burial plot instead of pontificating on my chosen profession.

Not long ago, when I was asked to spend a semester teaching a journalism course at Southern Methodist University, I felt for the most part that I was yelling down a dark hole. Using my old war stories as examples, I couldn't, in good conscious, promise any of my students that a newspaper job awaited them. I felt I was offering an impossible dream and couldn't blame them for doodling and checking their emails while I lectured.

Lordy, how times have changed. When I was their age, you had your pick since newspapers abounded and those who filled their staffs were vagabonds by nature. If a paper down the road offered a slight raise or a more appealing assignment, you loaded up the U-Haul and hit the road. The kindly and desperate managing editor of the *Roswell Daily Record* hired me after a single, long-distance phone conversation, sight unseen.

Careers were measured in stepping stones. You started at a small paper and took a job at one a bit larger and willing to add that five to ten dollars to your weekly salary, all the while hoping that someone at one of the even larger, more prestigious publications took notice of your remarkable talent and work ethic.

Today, that road map is no longer relevant. That entry level position on the surviving small papers is now being applied for by the experienced, over-qualified big city reporter who was recently laid off and, for whatever reason, wants to remain in the business.

I wish I had better news.

Be aware that the trail of mistakes I personally made in the dawning of my career would get you to Granny's house and back. And the veteran reporter sitting at the next desk didn't always prove to be the most ideal example.

One Sunday, I was serving as an eager assistant to the fellow worker whose responsibility it was to lay out the sports pages for the next morning's edition. I'll not mention his name but say only that he was quite talented and easily bored.

Since summer Sundays were quiet times on the local scene, determining what to publish for the Monday morning reader was a no-brainer. There were the results of Major League Baseball games and the final round of the weekly PGA tournament.

On this particular day, an unknown golfer named Miller Barber had a miraculous final round and won his first professional tournament. So low-key was the obscure Barber that it was doubtful many in his hometown of Texarkana, Texas, even knew he played golf.

Our mischievous deskman seized the moment.

He went into a back room where photos, old and new, were filed and reached into a folder filled with publicity pictures of old-time western movie star Tom Mix. He selected an aged mug shot of the former cowboy actor with plastered down hair parted in the middle and heavy, dark rings under his eyes. (While at his mischief, he also moved all photos of our esteemed managing editor into a folder labeled "Francis, the Talking Mule," another fixture from a bygone movie era.)

Accompanying the next morning's article on the PGA tournament was Mix's picture, identified as surprise winner Miller Barber.

Though I'd played no part, I was a bit concerned the following day when our boss arrived. He sat at his desk silently reviewing the section, before saying, "Boy, ol' Miller Barber doesn't look much like an athlete, does he?"

It was all that was ever said on the matter.

And, in truth, I should have been used to my fellow worker's game playing. As the junior member of the staff, among my duties was to receive the handwritten results delivered by the local pro wrestling promoter. It was an easy job, just a couple of paragraphs to say that Big Chief Warpath had regained his world championship belt by defeating The Destroyer. Etc., etc., ad nauseam.

The same staff member who had subbed Tom Mix for Miller Barber would occasionally volunteer to write the brief wrestling report for me. Only later would I learn that when doing so, he would always invent a match that had never taken place, describing it in bloody and dramatic detail.

I recall no wrestling fan or even the promoter ever lodging a complaint.

Nor did readers of the weekly bowling column, another of my dreaded rookie responsibilities. The owner of the local bowling lanes would drop by a stack of forms showing the results of league play. Each team was sponsored by a local business.

My friend would come to my desk, flip through the forms and, every so often, send me home early, saying he'd write the column. I never questioned his intent and beat a hasty trail for the door.

It was sometime later when I finally learned the reason for his generosity: he was always looking for a particular result. And if he could, in all honesty, write that "Team So-and-So beat Watson's Meat," he jumped at the opportunity. Think about it for a minute.

He was back on the desk laying out pages when it came time to preview the upcoming Kentucky Derby. The Associated Press's photo department had transmitted head shots of each of the twelve horses scheduled to start the race. My deskman friend looked them over carefully, then ordered twelve one-column prints—all of the same horse. In the following morning's edition, the photo of a single horse was published twelve times, with a different name beneath each of the photo.

Just as our staff jokester promised, no one noticed. A horse is a horse is a . . .

Finally, there was the late night when I returned to the office after a long-delayed game and was on a tight deadline. The ancient Underwood upright at my desk had suddenly decided to malfunction. It took only one loud curse for the happy prankster to come running.

When he recognized my dilemma, he volunteered to help and rushed off to the photo lab in search of a screwdriver. I watched for several minutes as he completely dismantled the cranky machine before throwing up his hands. "There's no way to fix it," he said as he pulled over a metal wastebasket and began tossing the parts into it. Sucked into the crime, I took the remains out the back door and tossed them into a trash bin. Upon my return, a functioning typewriter sat on my desk—swiped from the paper's absent religion writer.

Not exactly professional journalism at its finest, but, hey, the business was a lot more fun in those days.

As to my game-playing fellow worker, his hand was never called for any of his outrageous escapades, not even when the tearful church editor reported her typewriter stolen.

He finally left the business and became quite successful in public relations.

I've long wondered why someone hasn't written a book detailing the zany antics and ribald lifestyle of yesterday's sportswriters. No wonder those on the other end of the newsroom called ours the Toy Department.

Before my time, there was a well-known writer whose only shortcoming was his love of single malt. Making certain his flask was full before heading out for the press box was an important part of his pre-game preparation. A beloved sort, his adoptive fellow writers always kept watch on him to be sure he was still alert and sober enough to file his after-game story. If not, someone would write it for him. He had those kinds of friends.

Assigned to cover the New Year's Day Cotton Bowl, he had been enthusiastically celebrating the holiday long before kickoff. By half-time, he confided to a fellow journalist that he didn't think he was going to make it to the final gun. Sure enough, by the end of the third quarter his head was on his typewriter. He was sound asleep, snoring gently.

In those days, stories were typewritten, then handed page by page to a waiting Western Union operator who would hurriedly retype the accounts and deliver them along to the waiting newspaper.

Once everyone had finished sending their stories and packing up notebooks and typewriters, they helped their drunk-as-a-skunk friend to his feet, drove him to his downtown hotel room, and gently tucked him into bed.

In the wee hours of the morning, there came a loud knock at his door by an employee who said he had an urgent telegram from his office. Still not in the best of shape, the awakened sportswriter stumbled to the door to accept the telegram.

Its message was brief and to the point: "FIFTH STORY BEST (stop). FOR GOD'S SAKE STOP!"

Then, there were the war games rival papers liked to play. As the story goes, two San Antonio papers, both battling for circulation in outlying communities, knew one of the best ways to lure new readers was to be certain their local high school football games were regularly reported. The larger, more solvent of the two, arranged for stringers in each little town, paying a few bucks to those who phoned in results.

In time, *Paper A* began to suspect that the crosstown rival was waiting until its Friday night edition came off the presses, then would steal and rewrite the short regional reports. *Paper B* insisted it was doing no such thing.

The accusers devised a rather diabolical plan. It invented Agua Dulce High School and a star running back named Albert Stuneros.

Through the remainder of the season, the heroics of Agua Dulce and young Albert appeared regularly—in both papers. As the wins piled up, Stuneros's mythical statistics grew more and more impressive. In one game, he scored a half dozen touchdowns, in the first half, then played in the band during intermission.

While *Paper A* had its proof that its pages were weekly being pirated, it took its sweet time making a case since the charade had become so much fun. Too, it had a big ending in mind.

Aware that the offending paper annually picked and published a postseason All–Iron Man schoolboy team, it fashioned a press release on Agula Dulce High letterhead, listing all of Stuneros's academic and athletic achievements. So impressed was the crosstown editor that Albert was not only picked to the dream team but was named its honorary captain. Accompanying the article was a publicity photo that had accompanied Stuneros's stunning resume. It was actually an old AP photo of some obscure California junior college running back.

The jig finally came to an end when the unknowing editor of *Paper B* received an invitation to speak at the Agua Dulce football banquet but couldn't find the town on any map. He was further made aware he'd been duped when he received a cryptic note in the mail, suggesting he see what he came up with when he spelled "Stuneros" backwards.

Go ahead, try it.

I've mentioned working nights at the *Austin American-Statesmen* back in my college years. Chief among my chores was to take calls on regional high school basketball games. The sports editor was adamant that the stories include the scoring totals of everyone who participated. Names, he loved saying, sold newspapers.

Invariably, some stringer would fail to collect the necessary statistical information before phoning. A fellow reporter, overseer of the paper's regional coverage for ages, knew his beat backward and forward. Aware of the boss's scrapbook journalism demands, he was always quick to lend a hand.

Looking over my shoulder, he would say something like, "Okay, Johnny Smith is their top scorer, so give him fifteen points . . . Let's figure Billy Jones got twelve and, maybe, a dozen rebounds . . . Willie Brown almost always fouls out, so he gets eight . . . Jackie Ray usually comes off the bench and scores a bucket or two so let's give him six points . . ." He would go through the lineups of each team, building an imaginary box score that perfectly matched up with the final score. A pretty amazing trick, really.

The boss was happy, I was a little baffled by our inventive journalism, and, apparently, the readers were satisfied.

It's my best guess that there are hundreds of similar tales from those golden days.

For all the above-mentioned high living, heavy drinking, and game playing, there has long been a newspaper truism I'll sternly vouch for. Regardless of the name on the masthead of your favorite paper, you can count on its finest writing being found in the sports pages.

It was, after all, Bud Shrake and Gary Cartwright, a pair of acclaimed authors and screenwriters, who, in their earlier days as sportswriters, came up with Ricky Ron and Dickey Don, the famous Yewbet twins who were constantly entered in track meets all over the state but never showed up. Even after the public address announcer repeatedly requested that they immediately report to the starting area or be scratched from the race.

A warning: do not try any of these shenanigans at home or in the office. It is best those freewheeling, goof-off days are now history. One can enjoy his work without acting like Peter Pan.

For the most part, I learned a great deal and improved my skills as my career wound through stops in Abilene, Roswell, Lubbock, Amarillo, and finally Dallas, where I eventually moved up to the job of covering the Dallas Cowboys. It was the beat every sportswriter in Texas craved.

Life got no better, at least for a time.

Accidental Crime Writer

———

WHEN I FINALLY BEGAN to grow weary of deadline journalism, my mood increasingly darkened by a new boss imported from Back East, I began pondering a new course. Press box hotdogs, six weeks of college dorm living during annual summer training camps, and repeatedly asking young athletes to explain the complexities of the flex defense and two-minute offense in a language Joe Fan could understand had run their course. Too, my spot in the company parking lot was far from ideal.

I was looking for reasons to make a change even before I really knew it.

What I wanted to do was seek out those stories that would allow me to explore the widest range of human emotion possible. I hadn't a clue what that really meant or where to look for it. All I knew for certain was that it would involve finding ordinary people in interesting places who were suddenly faced with extraordinary circumstances, dramatic situations, and stories that would interest me as well as a wide range of readers.

But who were they? And where to find them?

The answer came during a visit from an old high school buddy who stopped by for dinner one evening. Ned Butler and I had been classmates in high school before we both accepted track scholarships to the University of Texas. I loved the place; he didn't. We'd lost touch only after he decided to transfer to the University of Texas at El Paso to join its football team. Later, he attended law school, and while I was bouncing from one Texas newsroom to another, he had become an assistant district attorney in nearby Waco.

As we sat on the back porch, reminiscing and enjoying the evening breeze, he told me of a case he would soon be trying, a murder of three teenagers whose bodies had been found in a park near Lake Waco. He spoke quietly of the victims, two girls and a boy, of those involved in the commission of the crime, of still-grieving family members, and of a dedicated law enforcement officer who had painstakingly sorted out a bizarre sequence of events that led to his solving of the crime.

The story haunted and fascinated me long after Ned left for home. It had the elements I was searching for, a cast of characters whose lives had be thrown together by the cruelest of fates.

Though I had never even seen the inside of a courtroom before and had little previous interest in the workings of the criminal justice system, I drove daily to attend the six-week trial. And there I found what I had been searching for.

And I realized I had a lengthy and demanding journey ahead. Two years, in fact. No one, myself included, can fully realize the demands of such an undertaking.

Giles Tippette, my longtime writing friend, had been interviewed by a magazine and was asked about the financial rewards of his chosen profession. It caused him to launch into a bit of a misinformed rant. Without mentioning any names, he bemoaned the fact "a friend who writes true crime books and earns a handsome fee for his effort." And all this "friend" had to do was sit through a trial, take notes, then rush back to his typewriter and pound away.

I called Giles to try and educate him. He, in turn, insisted it was another "friend" he'd been referring to. I took him at his word, and we remained pals.

In my learn-on-the-fly experience, the trial offers little more than an outline of the story one will attempt to tell. It provides only a timeline of critical events and a cast of the main characters—the judge, lawyers, defendant, witnesses, and those interested observers who regularly take their places in the gallery.

In time, people involved will become curious as to who you are and what your interest is in the event. Thus begins the get-acquainted process. But far too soon to request interviews. It is, however, an excellent opportunity to gather physical descriptions, note mannerisms, and collect personality traits simply by being a silent observer. Since all trials have a good deal of idle time, casual hallway conversations are certain to occur, even occasional invitations to visit the court-house coffee shop. There is nothing more valuable in the fact-gathering process than having your subjects become comfortable with your presence—and being patient.

If the latter is a problem, it is a good sign you've taken on a project you're really not suited for. Make certain you're excited enough about your subject to stick with it over a long haul.

For example, the mother of one of the victims was obviously wary of all media. Though she was aware of my reason for being at the trial daily, her warming process was glacially slow. But as fate would have it, she and my wife, Pat, hit it off and began to occasionally have lunch together. Ultimately, I was invited to join them for casual conversation. She had to know that I hoped to interview her about the horrific experience she'd been put through, but clearly the time was not right.

A personal rule I've held to regarding interviews is not one most editors and fellow journalists embrace. If a subject declines my request, I respect that decision, accept it as a final word, and go elsewhere in search of needed information. The timing, then, is vital if one hopes to avoid the dreaded turndown.

In the case of the mother, she had become comfortable enough to even occasionally visit in our home long after the trial had ended, but we never spoke of things I badly wished to ask her.

Months passed before she phoned one morning and invited me to her home. "I'm ready," she said. Our subsequent discussions about her lost child, how she had learned of the murder, and her initial response were part of one of the most emotional interviews I've ever done. And I'm certain it would have never taken place without the proper passage of time.

It was to her that I delivered the first copy of the finished book my publisher provided me. Her positive response was another lesson learned. Upon publication of each new book, I would request early copies from the publisher to personally distribute to the families of the victims. It didn't seem right for them to first see it in some bookstore window or newspaper ad.

The father of one of the murdered girls refused to attend the trial and had early on made it clear he would be doing no interviews. Thus, the book was written without his direct input. Still, I visited him with an early copy of the finished product, acknowledging that I knew he was unlikely to ever open it.

A few days later he called. "I've just finished reading your book," he said, "and I'm very pleased with the way you portrayed my daughter. Thank you."

It was as fine a review as I hoped to receive and the last conversation we would ever have. But it meant a great deal to me.

Along the way, there was also an ex-girlfriend of one of the convicted killers. Though I'd never even met her, I knew she was aware that I was writing the book. She had moved somewhere out of state, and I had long since given up hope of learning her rare insight. Until she also phoned to tell me she had decided to talk with me if I was interested.

Interested? It took reservations on three separate airlines to get to her location, but I managed to be there the following day. The trip and months of waiting were well worth it.

Over the years, I've become convinced that if you display the proper degree of professionalism, a touch of genuine humility, and a willingness to go the extra mile to get to the truth, nothing but the truth, you're going to make friends along the way.

Years later, I was working on *Open Secrets* when I learned that Joy Aylor, the woman who had managed to stay one step ahead of law enforcement for months, was finally located and arrested in Vence, France, a picturesque mountainside village near Nice. Thank goodness I had a passport.

Neither an experienced international traveler nor fluent in any language other than Texan, I was on my way.

With no real plan of attack, I first visited an English-speaking editor at *Paris Match* and, best as I could, explained the reason for my visit. He had been aware of the arrest and, in fact, asked if I might write him a piece on the events that had led to it when I returned home. Which, of course, I agreed to do, having never been published in French before. He also provided direction to the Nice police station. After making a couple of calls, he said it was his understanding that a detective named Huy Decloedt had made the arrest.

I arrived at the police department the next day, silently hoping that I'd find someone who spoke English. (I'd considered finding an interpreter but hadn't had time.)

Escorted into a brightly lit room filled with the smells of cigarettes and stale coffee, I hurriedly began explaining the purpose for my unannounced visit.

A slightly built Vietnamese man, dressed in jeans, casual shirt, and tennis shoes, got to his feet and walked my way. Detective Decloedt wasn't smiling, but at least he spoke English. "It is our policy not to give interviews to reporters," he said, loud enough for everyone in the room to hear. With that, he turned back to his desk.

End of conversation.

I was in the parking lot, almost to my rental car, when I heard him call out. He approached and, still not showing even a hint of a smile, asked where I was staying. "My wife and I will have dinner with you at the hotel tonight at eight o'clock," he said, then turned back to the building.

That evening, he described the dramatic arrest in minute detail and recounted his conversation with his prisoner on their drive back into Nice and those he'd had with her since she'd been jailed. He confided that she had attempted suicide in her cell and was currently under a doctor's care. There would be no chance of my interviewing her. Still, thanks to him, I judged my trip a roaring success.

Our dinner went late into the night, and as I walked with him and his wife to their car, I told him I had one final question: What had prompted his decision to go against policy and talk with me?

He shrugged as if the answer was obvious. "Any journalist who would travel as far as you have to do his work must be quite serious about it," he said.

Sometime after my trip, I told of my experience to the Dallas County attorney who would prosecute the case. After I shared some of the information I'd learned, he immediately contacted Detective Decloedt and persuaded him to come to America and testify during Aylor's trial.

Upon his arrival, we again had dinner. Decloedt had brought a bottle of wine, and we spent the evening like old friends.

It has been my experience that most who are involved in a traumatic, life-changing event—loved ones of victims as well as investigators—do want to talk about it. Part of what an author is doing is providing them a public forum. They just need to speak out on their own terms, in their own good time and place. It is a mindset well worth honoring.

My talks with the mother and girlfriend were but a couple of over one hundred interviews done to get a firmer grasp of the Waco story. And, yes, it was information initially gathered during the trial that provided my entrée.

Yet, recounting the trial was the final chapter of the twenty-four-month project, the book's last pages. It was not filled with a droning visit to testimony or a roll call of the witness parade but, rather, one recalling the color, drama, and emotion. And, of course, the verdict and the reaction it generated.

The writer who attempts to tell his crime story armed with nothing but endless courtroom questions and answers is the same person who would likely choose to ride a motorcycle through the Louvre.

So, you've now attended the trial and acquainted yourself with the basics of the story and its main characters. You've seen the map and feel a welcome degree of comfort in the fact you (a) have some grasp of your mission and (b) are now confident that your planned story has the dramatic elements you'd hoped to find.

There is also a sense of great relief that the jury has returned a guilty verdict. Without it, there is no book. Underline that, highlight it, repeat it three times quickly. There is an unwritten rule in the publishing world that any potential true crime book without a satisfactory justice-is-served ending simply won't fly (unless, of course, you were among the legions who attended the O. J. Simpson trial). While most rules are made to be broken, you're most likely spending a great deal of wasted effort researching a crime story that lacks a tied-in-a-bow ending.

With a new degree of enthusiasm once you do, in fact, have your ending, you have the urge to begin writing. Forget it. The work is just beginning, and every answered question begs a half dozen others. Trust me, I learned the hard way. After one miserable attempt to write a chapter too soon, I tossed it aside and spent the next year gathering information. I visited the crime scene, gravesites, and traveled routes I would later need to describe, anything that would help me put the reader there. It seemed I was constantly on the road.

Naturally, interviews consumed the greatest amount of time. And, almost without exception, any conversation I had pointed to others who I had not previously planned to speak with. Slowly at first, then in high gear, the story took control. At times, I felt I was simply following along, trying to keep up.

Once comfortable that you know the basics—how you will get from beginning to middle to end—it is time to prepare a proposal, your sales tool. Few serious writers will take on such a massive project on spec, writing a 100,000-word manuscript with no commitment from a publisher. Many have tried, most have failed, never to write again. Unless you've had success with the lottery or a rich uncle, it is imperative that a publisher be willing to advance some financing to help defray the cost of your time away from other money-making projects. Even with the book advance, one most likely will find need to accept shorter, quicker-paying magazine assignments from time to time.

But, back to the proposal, an important art form that remains something of a mystery to me. One school of thought holds that it should be brief, ten to twelve pages at most, to fit the busy attention span of its editor/reader. Others will tell you that it should be three times that long, highly detailed, accompanied by a sample chapter or two and an outline that makes one think back on freshman English.

The latter demand is, to me, absurd inasmuch as you will not yet have enough information to completely describe the myriad twists and turns the plot is certain to take. That would take shape only after you've done all your research and interviews.

How, then, are you to know early in the game that a particular person will become more interesting and important than you'd previously assumed, how one seemingly minor event sets off a chain reaction of other occurrences that become vital? For instance, who would have known that along the way I would encounter a fascinating young woman who claimed psychic abilities and insisted she had experienced a disturbing (and pretty accurate) vision of the murders?

Boastful though it might sound, I can honestly say that over the years I've routinely delivered better books than were promised by any of my proposals.

Inasmuch as this adventure remains among my admitted short-comings, it would be best to consult with your literary agent for guidance. He or she knows the editors they plan to pitch your project to and will have a better idea of their tastes and demands. Since the agent wants to sell your book almost as badly as you, careful editing of the proposal before it goes off to New York can be counted on.

I do know that the proposal, the pitch, should be carefully thought out and well crafted, regardless of length. It is what gets your foot in the door. And, in today's marketplace, it should be presented by an agent. We'll talk more about that later.

Despite all your well-written efforts to persuade an editor of the rare importance of your planned book, be prepared for disappointment. I could paper the wall with the rejections my first true crime effort generated, for reasons that included everything from the unfamiliar locale of the story to my being a relative unknown in publishing circles. Be aware that if your return address is somewhere out in the hinterland, zip codes removed from the Big Apple, your ability will always be suspect.

Here's been my proposal approach: in an effort to grab an editor's attention and quickly draw him or her into the story, I write the proposal much as I would a quick-read magazine piece, but in the voice that will be used in the subsequent book. Not only must it include details of the centerpiece crime, investigation, and legal outcome, but an introduction of the main characters, amount of publicity the story has received, and reasons the book will be salable and unique in a highly competitive genre. I attempt to anticipate any and all questions they might have and be sure they're addressed.

From it, an editor (and his marketing department) will determine if the project has merit (sales potential) and holds proof that you have the writing ability the project will require. On the basis of what amounts to a highlighted version of your story and how you plan to tell it, you will either be offered a contract or will get the dreaded "thanks, but not for us" response.

Finally, after months of waiting, a regional press was impressed enough to offer a modest advance (half to be paid upon signing the contract, the other upon acceptance of a completed manuscript) which I snapped up before they could change their mind. We wouldn't be living high on the hog in the days to come, but at least I had a signed and sealed commitment.

After months of travel, interviews, researching documents, then writing, revisions, and search for a title that felt right (I was determined that the word "blood," tritely used in so many true crime titles, absolutely not be considered), *Careless Whispers* finally went off to the publisher. And the unpredictable occurred.

Though Taylor Publishing had limited distribution capabilities, the book sold well, making local bestseller lists and receiving warm reviews. In record time, a second printing was ordered. A crowd of over five hundred turned out to a Waco mall bookstore one Saturday afternoon, resulting in a *Publishers Weekly* item and an accompanying photo showing the long lines at the signing.

Several national paperback houses made reprint bids for the book, offering advances well in excess of the numbers on my original contract. Pocket Books, one of the many who had originally turned its nose up at my proposal, ultimately bought the softcover rights, and other reprint offers came from publishers in Germany, Japan, and Great Britain. And it was soon optioned by a motion picture production company.

We weren't exactly on Easy Street, but the neighborhood was improving.

I must admit that at the time I knew nothing of the Mystery Writers of America or their annual presentations of Edgar Allan Poe Awards in a variety of categories. But, when I received notification that *Careless Whispers* was named one of the five finalists for the Best Fact Crime book of the year, I began my homework, learning that past winners included the likes of Truman Capote and his milestone *In Cold Blood.* Admittedly, the old sportswriter's ego shot up several degrees.

Skipping to the punchline: on a memorable evening in a New York ballroom, my book was announced as the winner of the highly regarded porcelain bust of Mr. Poe. No Super Bowl I'd ever covered could compare.

Suddenly, sitting beside my wife and editor, the coveted prize in hand, I became something I'd never set out to be. I was officially a true crime writer.

Later that night, back in our hotel room, I remember waking with the chilling thought that it had all been a dream. I slipped from the bed and quietly made my way through the darkness to a nearby dresser, and sure enough, there sat ol' Edgar. Thereafter, I slept soundly.

In days to come, I suggested a variety of nonfiction subjects for my next book. Some of the ideas, as I recall, weren't too shabby. But the response of everyone from my new agent to editors was always the same: I should write another true crime book.

So, of course, I did. In two-year increments, I wrote a half dozen, making every effort to tell stories that involved different types of situations and protagonists. One followed the heroic efforts of a female detective (*To the Last Breath*), and another dealt with the murder of a young police officer working undercover in a rural high school (*Innocence Lost*). Yet another revisited the investigation and solving of a series of fifteen-year-old crimes by a determined young investigator in the local DA's office (*Scream at the Sky*). Each book told a unique story.

And, lo and behold, in 1999, a decade after publication of *Careless Whispers*, I was back in New York as *To the Last Breath* also received the Edgar. I got as much a kick out of it as did an inscription writer pal Kent Biffle, who later wrote to me in his wonderful collection of newspaper columns: "To my Old Friend," he wrote. "One Edgar is Wonderful. Two is a bit swinish . . ."

The books' only similarity was that each was set in Texas. I knew my homeland, its mindsets and manners, its landscape and lifestyles, and only felt comfortable writing about it. When asked if I might be interested in a faraway case, I pled to being a homebody and declined.

There's an old and frayed writers' tale that involves a conversation that goes something like this:

"Amazing, isn't it, that old so-and-so has now written fifty books?"

"What's even more amazing is that he's managed to write the same book fifty times."

I didn't want to become the subject of that kind of joke, so I chose my stories carefully. To invest months and years on a project demands a great deal of sustained energy and enthusiasm. For me, seeking out unique stories was essential.

While we're still using *Careless Whispers* as our textbook, perhaps this is a good time to visit the wonderful world of Hollywood. It is my general opinion that it is a land of smoke, mirrors, and enough grade A bullshit to fertilize all the cotton fields in my native state.

I was paying a visit to the Cowboys' summer training camp in Thousand Oaks, California, when a woman representing the production company that had optioned the book caught up with me. She couldn't have been more excited to hear my voice. Since I was already "on the Coast," she wanted to know if it would be possible for me to come into Los Angeles for a meeting to discuss the project. Their office, she announced, was on the Universal Studios lot. She would leave my name at the gate.

Welcome to the Big Time, Old Sport.

Upon my arrival, I was told repeatedly how absolutely wonderful my book was. The movie was going to be big, really big. Who did I see playing the role of the deputy who solved the case? I think someone let the word genius slip a time or two. We had lunch in the Universal commissary, where several familiar stars in costume and munching on sandwiches nearby were pointed out to me. I even shook the hand of a TV sitcom actress.

Back in the office they wanted me to be certain my book was in good hands. I was given a video tape cassette of a movie they had recently produced, *The Burning Bed*, starring Farrah Fawcett. "We want you to see the quality of our work," I was told.

The meeting ended with an "our people will be in touch with your people" promise and handshakes all around. I drove away, seeing my name in lights.

Then time passed. A week, then a month with no word. My agent reminded me that this sort of thing happened all the time. The option I'd agreed to was for one year, so there was plenty of time for something to happen—if it was going to.

After another silent month or so, I'd pretty well removed movie making from my bucket list and began researching a new book.

But, finally, a letter bearing the production company's return address arrived. Better late than never, I thought, as I ripped into the envelope and read a one-sentence note:

"Dear Mr. Stowers. Would you be so kind as to return the copy of *The Burning Bed*, which we lent you when you visited our office?"

From that, the ol' writer from Hicksville learned his lesson. Fool me once . . . I decided I'd just as soon deal with the mob, who I could only assume would be more honest and straightforward.

When their option finally expired, yet another production company purchased it for another modest fee. Found money, my agent pointed out. Don't get too excited. After their year ran out, a third group stepped up. I happily deposited their check with no expectations. Even when I was alerted that the book had been turned over to a screenwriter who was hard at work, I felt no real tingle.

And, sure enough, that option period also came to a sad, silent end. Finally, there were no more interested buyers.

I was completing *Innocence Lost*, a book about the undercover officer who had been shot and killed by the sixteen-year-old son of a policeman. The crime had occurred outside the small community of Midlothian, just a fifteen-minute drive from my house. It, too, had been a project that consumed another fascinating two years of my life.

Out of the blue came a phone call from Dan Witt, the man who had ordered the forgotten screenplay for *Careless Whispers*. He wanted to know if the book was still under option.

When I told him it wasn't, he explained that actor Robert Conrad was under contract to CBS to do three movies. If he didn't do the third one before a fast-approaching deadline, he would be forced to return a considerable sum to the network. Witt asked if I would mind him showing Conrad his script?

Why not? We bothered with no contract, no "his people-my people" discussions. Dan was a fellow Texan; that was good enough for me.

Soon, however, it became necessary for my agent, Conrad's lawyers, and CBS executives to put their heads together. I stayed as far removed as I could.

Less than a month after Witt's call, production was underway. I had signed an agreement that would pay me the going rate for a two-hour Movie of the Week. The title had been changed to *Sworn to Vengeance*. It aired to a sizable audience, including my wife and me who watched from the comfort of our living room, and has been reshown in late-night spots several times over the years.

So, the moral of the story: be aware that the road from book to movie is filled with potholes, dead ends, and disappointments. Ah, but there is always that element of pure luck one shouldn't overlook. If an actor hadn't been in a jam, if Dan Witt hadn't known of the problem and that a script had been written, and ready to be shot, if the book had still been under option to fly-by-night Graveyard Productions, nothing would have ever happened. In the end, it was one of those unexpected strikes of lightening.

There were no Emmys won, no series spin-offs, but I must admit to feeling a quiet satisfaction. Of the five books that had been finalists for the Edgar back in 1986, all had been made into movies. Leading the parade was Nicholas Peliggi's Academy Award–winning *Goodfellas*, based on his excellent book *Wise Guys: Life in a Mafia Family*. The rest of us had to settle for the small screen.

As I watched *Sworn to Vengeance* that evening, I liked the script, I liked the actors, and I very much liked seeing something I had written adapted to another medium, strange though it might be. It didn't even bother me too much that they chose to replace the real-life male district attorney with a female.

I'll not bother sharing the number of wannabe authors with a story in mind that they're dead certain would not only be a bestselling book but a great movie. Their friends have assured them of as much. I guess Stephen King does, but I suspect there are precious few others who begin writing a book, fiction or nonfiction, intending for it to be coming to a theater near you. If that's your plan, stock up on antidepressants.

As of this writing, I have had numerous books optioned, sometimes even with a bit of fanfare. Those flames generally died very quickly. I've done no research on the matter, but I'm betting for every optioned book that actually becomes a movie, TV, or theatrical, there are ten thousand—probably more—that are forgotten for whatever reason.

I've been enormously fortunate. *Open Secrets* actually became a two-part ABC miniseries titled *Telling Secrets*, starring Cybil Sheppard and Ken Olan. And, full disclosure, there was again a bit of luck involved. My friend Dan Witt, who had rescued *Careless Whispers*, liked the story, championed it, and eventually became one of its producers.

As they say, sometimes it's not what you know, but who.

An exciting side note moment from all that came when Jennifer Miller, who had written the screenplay for *Telling Secrets*, was nominated for an Emmy for another movie she'd done. She was unable to attend the televised award ceremonies, so when her name was called, her photograph, taken by my wife during one of her research visits, appeared on the screen. That's the closest either of us has ever been to the Hollywood red carpets.

A decade has now passed since publication of my last true crime book. I'm regularly asked why I decided to turn to other subjects and when I will wise up and get back to the genre that earned me some measure of recognition and success. And why turn away in the first place?

There is a simple answer and one a bit more difficult to explain.

The quick explanation is that the market for true crime books went into drastic decline at the end of the '90s as a deluge of reality-based TV shows emerged. Suddenly, the public appetite could be satisfied simply by sitting in an easy chair and flipping channels.

Generally, it worked this way: some production assistant would be assigned to run down to Barnes & Noble or Half Price Books and gather all the true crime books available, pick out an interesting one, then reach out to the author. He would be told that the show was planning a segment on a case he had written a really super book about, and boy howdy, it would be just wonderful if you would be willing to sit for an interview. They would even promise, cross their hearts, that they would show the cover of your book on air. Imagine the sales that would generate.

For a while, I fell for it. A camera crew would invade my office, stringing wires, setting up lights, and rearranging furniture. The host had his or her questions arranged (after having read your book, of course). It was usually a day long process. And once the finished product, featuring cheesy recreations played out by novice actors, aired, your book got maybe ten seconds of airtime. The tedious day of answering questions as the cameras rolled was boiled down to a couple of minutes. It finally dawned on me they were mining for information their own script writer could use.

If the shows helped sell a single book, I was never aware of it. Nor was I ever compensated for my time and input.

Finally, the country boy wised up and learned to say no after finally realizing he was party to his own professional decline. Once-brisk book sales had begun to decline and, with rare exception, those still being published were quickly written paperbacks for which the author received considerably less up-front money.

It didn't take a math whiz to see that the days of a multiyear commitment to a project were history. Thus, I had a built-in excuse for a career change.

In truth, my primary reason was that I had grown weary of my viewing gross inhumanity, wandering endlessly through the dark side of society in a futile attempt to understand it. Maybe the reader could remain at arm's length, but not the writer. I had met wonderful people along the way, friends forever, but I increasingly abhorred the events that had brought us together.

I was all but certain that my crime-writing career was over when a call came one evening from a young woman in Wichita Falls. Was I, she asked, the author of *Careless Whispers*? After acknowledging that I was, she explained that her older sister had been a close friend of Raylene Rice, one of the long-ago Waco victims. Later, her sister had also been a murder victim along with four other young women. Now, after fourteen years, it appeared the killer had finally been arrested. Would I be interested in writing about it?

Reluctantly, I agreed to drive to Wichita Falls and meet with her.

If I'd had a daughter, I would have wished her to be like Catie Reid. Pretty, charming, and beneath her warm, vibrant smile was an almost tangible strength. I listened to her story, met another sister and her aunt, saw photographs of the victim in life, and heard praise for a quiet investigator who had solved the cases and become the family's savior.

By the time I left her house, I knew there would be one more true crime stop before I could move on to more cheery subjects. I prepared the dreaded proposal which was apparently sufficient to pique the interest of my St. Martin's editor, Charlie Spicer. The advance he could offer was considerably shy of some he'd previously made, but he assured me the book would debut as a hardback.

For several months, Wichita Falls became my second home. The story I planned to tell was filled with bizarre twists, a Byzantine plot, and, again, fascinating people.

John Little, a former bricklayer who had finally solved the crime, had taken the investigator's post in the DA's office after being turned down by the local police because of poor eyesight. Long before he became involved in the case, another man had been tried for one of the murders but found innocent. The actual killer, Faryion Wardrip, was a prowling ghost who for years had hidden his anger in substance abuse and violent fantasies.

And there was Catie Reid who, though barely a teenager when her big sister was killed, had for years displayed the strength that held her family together. It was she who could not rest until there was justice.

The end result was *Scream at the Sky*.

Soon after publication of the book, Catie called and asked if I would consider one more trip to Wichita Falls. Her aunt was coming from California to visit, and they would like to take me to lunch. "I'm so proud of the book you wrote and don't know any other way to say thank you," she told me.

How do you say no to an invitation like that?

It was a delightful reunion. The conversation was upbeat and cheerful, with no mention of the tragic events that had initially brought us together. After lunch, Catie drove us out to a nearby lake lot she and her husband had just purchased and on which they planned to build a house.

By the time I left to return home, I was in great spirits, particularly pleased to see how Catie had finally begun to put her dark past aside and happily focus on a brighter future.

I had been home only a brief time when her aunt phoned. Her voice was barely a whisper, the lilt I'd heard just a few hours earlier gone. "Catie was killed in a car accident an hour ago," she said before breaking into sobs that I can only describe as chilling. I was at a loss for words.

My next trip, then, was to attend a funeral.

Following the church service, I rode to the cemetery with the district attorney Barry Macha. He, too, had greatly admired Catie Reid's remarkable strength and resolve. Neither of us spoke as we approached the gravesite, yet I was certain we were both lost in similar thoughts.

At times, in a world filled with cruel and ugliness, there is no justice.

For some time afterwards, I felt a gnawing emptiness. And I found myself questioning my career path even more. What had just happened made absolutely no sense to me, and I had no tools to explain such an unfair death. What business did I have writing of tragedy after tragedy when its reason escaped me?

That unanswered question was the reason for my decision to write no more true crime books. The time had come for me to heed the final words I'd painfully written in *Sins of the Son*, a book about my imprisoned son who, in a drug-fueled rage, had murdered his ex-wife.

"There comes a time, in matters of the heart, when one must set aside the anger and disappointments and seek the warmth that drives away the cold and, finally, begins to soften the bad with the good."

With that in mind, I headed to Penelope, Texas, a place I'd never heard of, where none of its 211 residents could recall the last time a crime had occurred in their little town There, I wanted to explore a simpler and all but forgotten lifestyle.

East of West

MY PLAN, still in the formulative stage, was to focus on the tiny farm town's school and its beloved yet beleaguered six-man football team, to describe a wholesome, can-do way of life that too many of us had forgotten or never known. I wanted to introduce readers to a hardscrabble, paycheck-to-paycheck, good folks' community, and Penelope seemed perfect.

My agent warned that it would be a hard sell. Still, he queried ten publishers and finally found one, Da Capo Press, willing to take the gamble. One was all I needed.

I walked into an atmosphere that was welcoming and refreshing. The superintendent, Harley Johnson, opened all doors. I could visit classrooms, wander the halls, attend practices, and talk with anyone willing to give me a few minutes. Such an attitude can only be found among those who have rarely, if ever, been exposed to the media.

So, I was back to school, arriving daily after a fifty-mile drive, getting to know the people I would write about. There was Johnson's part-time secretary, Gloria Walton, owner of the local grain mill and volunteer sponsor of Penelope High's award-winning one-act play program. Cory McAdams had learned his coaching trade at knee of his legendary father and drove forty-five miles to work daily. His wife, April, taught in the elementary school. One of the cheerleader's grandfather had donated the land on which the nearby football field had been built by local volunteers.

I learned that the Penelope Independent School District was, at the time, the sixteenth poorest in the entire state yet found inventive ways to accommodate its students. If there was a course for which there was no teacher, arrangements were made to virtually visit a classroom at nearby Hillsboro's Hill College. When several students expressed an interest in having a tennis team (at a school without a single tennis court), a teacher volunteered to drive the youngsters to Waco twice a week for practice on the Baylor University courts. They won the district championship.

Their game of six-man football had been invented by a Chester, Nebraska, teacher in the mid-1930s and was currently played in Texas by high schools with enrollments of ninety-nine students or less. Their final scores often sounded more like results of a fast-pace basketball game. Almost weekly during the season some team would score as many as one hundred points.

Penelope, I quickly realized, was a kids-come-first kind of place. When the ragtag Wolverines played on Friday nights, everyone turned out in support. Many had a designated role. Karen Osborne, mother of one of the cheerleaders, sang the national anthem a cappella, English instructor Mike Baker served as the public address announcer, and mothers of the players worked the concession stand. Their husbands fired up barbecue grills to provide those who had paid their three-dollar admission fee with hamburgers and hotdogs. Teacher Paula Harlin baked cupcakes and cookies that were sold to raise money for a new telescope for science class.

In a state that worships high school football, where million-dollar stadiums and six-figure coaching salaries are not uncommon, Penelope's program operated on limited funds. Few complained.

My admiration of the people and enthusiasm for my project grew with each visit.

I followed the team's weekly effort to win a game, visiting rival outposts like Cranfills Gap, Oglesby, and Aquilla, occasionally stopping in at a Malone honky-tonk where Penelope resident David Lednicky and his country band performed. I visited in homes and watched people vote and speak out at school board meetings. I was even invited to be guest speaker at the school's athletic banquet.

On days when I was at home in not the best of moods for whatever reason, Pat had a simple solution. "Penelope's got a volleyball game tonight. Why don't you take a drive down and watch it?" she would suggest, knowing the visit was certain to lift my spirits.

One after-school evening, while visiting Superintendent Johnson, I asked what kept him in Penelope, constantly battling financial woes and long hours.

He answered by telling a story.

"A couple of years ago, I had this young man sitting in my office as punishment for acting up in class. He was a loner, with few friends, and didn't participate in any of our extracurricular activities. He walked to school alone every morning, head down, wearing a hooded sweatshirt. He and his single mom lived in a mobile home over near the post office.

"While he was sitting there, I received a phone call. The boy's mother had just been killed in a car accident on the way home from Hillsboro. It would not only be my responsibility to pass along the terrible news but to also determine how to care for the student.

"He seemed in a daze after I'd told him the tragic news. The only relative he had was an uncle in Waco who he barely knew.

"In a little place like this, news, good and bad, travels fast. Soon, the mother of another of our students called and volunteered to immediately take the boy into their home.

"For the next couple of days, several of our students, kids who really didn't know the young man, visited him to express their sympathy and show support.

"When time came for the funeral, I was surprised at how many of our young people attended.

"As the service was about to begin, I noticed that the boy was sitting alone on the front row. Our other kids, most who probably had never attended a funeral before, were sitting together in the pews near the back of the church.

"Then, however, something amazing happened. One by one, they began walking down to the front to sit with the grieving youngster. I'd never seen anything like it. It moved me to tears.

"That," he concluded, "is why I stay here."

And it was why I wrote *Where Dreams Die Hard*.

In all honesty I had little hope that a book on such an under-the-radar topic might enjoy any success.

A call just a week or so after its publication once again demonstrated how little I knew of the publishing world. The editor the *New York*

Times op-ed pages had just read the book and asked if I would write a piece for him on Penelope and six-man football. It would be cleverly titled "Friday Night Lites."

Texas Monthly, which had never taken notice of my efforts before, gave it a nice review, saying reading it was "like paying a visit to a country relative."

Superintendent Johnson suggested a book signing in the school gym. I contacted Da Capo and was impressed when told the press would like to donate two hundred copies to the Penelope ISD. Every copy was sold.

The following fall, curious fans from as far away as Colorado Springs, Colorado, attended Wolverine games. The athletic director of the University Oklahoma called me one Sunday morning and said he'd bet I couldn't guess where he was. On the way home from a weekend meeting, he had detoured to visit the Penelope football field. "I'm standing on the fifty-yard line right now," he said.

Several months later, after a horrific industrial explosion occurred in nearby West, President Barack Obama came to Texas to pay homage to the town and those who had lost loved ones. The culmination of his visit would be a nationally televised speech in Waco.

Later that day, April McAdams called to ask if I had watched the speech. If not, she said, she was sending me a link to the introductory remarks that had been given by Baylor president Kenneth Starr.

I watched and listened as much of his brief welcome to the president was spent referring to the remarkable community spirit of people like those portrayed in a book he had just read about neighboring Penelope, the little town east of West.

And, in time, *Dallas Morning News* book columnist Judy Alter ranked *Where Dreams Die Hard* among what she considered the ten all-time best books on Texas.

There comes a time in every author's life when someone will ask him to pick a favorite from all the books he's written. It's much like asking a father which of his children is his favorite. I have no such problem. My time spent in Penelope, Texas, has made my answer easy.

The Process

———

ATTEND ENOUGH WRITERS' CONFERENCES or read enough back issues of *Writers' Digest*, and you'll learn that the work habits of stay-at-home journalists and authors vary widely. One might only write in the wee hours of the night, after the wife and kids have finally gone to bed. Another is up at the crack of dawn, finishing a page or two before getting to the bottom of his first cup of coffee. Some set daily word count goals, others work a certain number of hours daily as if a taskmaster was watching over them.

Again, you'll find no set rule. Whatever works for you and gets the job done.

Now in my AARP years, I prefer the up-and-at-'em approach. In fact, the sun is not quite over the horizon as I begin writing this particular section.

So, here's my routine:

When working on a book, I first review what I'd written the previous day, editing and polishing, adding and subtracting. It normally won't be a wholesale rewrite, won't take more than forty-five minutes or so, and is intended to (a) clean up whatever messes I've left behind and (b) remind me of where I've been and where the story will go.

A neat little trick is to leave off today's writing at a point where you'll know where to begin the next day. If it's midsentence, so be it.

After making my revisions, it is time to put out seed for the birds and squirrels. I'm not one who can sit and stare at a computer screen for marathon stretches. Once I've stopped by the coffee pot, I get back to work.

If the writing gods are smiling, I work on the new material for an hour, maybe two.

Then it's time for a quick breakfast. And, oh yes, I need to check my emails. Sometimes I just like to pace or stand at the window, checking to make sure the critters outdoors are satisfied with their sunflower seeds.

Back to work, I make more headway until my sleepy-eyed terrier Max arrives in my office, insisting it is time for our thirty-minute walk to tend necessaries and make certain that all's well in the neighborhood.

More coffee when we return, then back to business. But, wait, wasn't I supposed to call and see if I can drop the car by for an oil change later in the day? I've got a million excuses.

Which is to say, I write in bursts and have invented every sneaky reason possible to take breaks. Corporate America would banish me from my cubicle before a week was out.

During those intermissions, however, I'm constantly thinking of what I want to write when I sit back down. And by midday I've usually accomplished my mission.

If a deadline is closing in or the creative juices are flowing, I might stay at my post longer than usual. But normally I'm done by no later than early afternoon, free to get that oil change or mow the yard. For me, an important signal to pay heed to is that time when the process begins to feel labored and my attention begins to wander. That's when quitting time has arrived.

In a determined effort to make satisfactory progress even when the clever phrases and vital information don't rush from my fingertips, I will sometimes stubbornly force the issue, even if aware that it isn't top-of-the-line work. I can make necessary amends when I review the next day.

So, you can write from midnight to dawn if that works for you. Tether yourself to a chair, lock your office door, and put in an eight-hour day (much of which will likely be spent staring slack-jawed at an empty screen). I'm just not hermit enough for such death march habits.

I wish I could remember the author about whom the following little tale was told.

Aware that he was having gridlock difficulties with his writing, a friend stopped in to check on his progress. "How did it go today?" the concerned visitor asked.

The troubled author shook his head. "I've been sitting here all day and only got three words written."

"Yeah, but I bet they were three good words."

"I'm not so sure. I can't determine what order they're supposed to go in."

At least he was trying.

For my money, the lamest excuse in the profession is "writer's block." I simply don't believe in such malady and challenge you to find it in any medical dictionary. Sure, there are days when the prose flows, then those when it might clunk ever so loudly. Think the guy who works a twelve-hour shift out at the water plant goes to work all bright-eyed and bushy-tailed every day? Just like him, you've got a job to do. If you're a writer, you write, be it good, bad, or even sometimes mud-fence ugly. But, it's how you ultimately make sure Max's Kibbles bowl stays full and the bills don't pile up.

The one plan I do stick to is this:

Whether you're writing a 3,000-word magazine article or an 85,000-word novel, you're going to be given a deadline by your editor. Get out your calendar and calculate how many working days you'll have before the manuscript is due. Then divide that number into the word length. Even one who failed to get past the multiplication tables can determine how many words daily he or she will need to turn out to get the work in on time.

Believe me when I say there is nothing more uplifting than that rare moment when you check your word count and find you are several thousand ahead of schedule and can afford to take off a day to watch a ballgame or see if the fish are biting.

In those too frequent times when you're running behind, the week-end gets shot all to hell and you use it to catch up. Hopefully, that will not become a standard practice since, I'm convinced, everyone deserves a carefree Saturday and Sunday.

That, however, may not be the case as you move your lengthier project along. Even when the computer is shut down and the lights in your office are off, the brain rarely rests. Wherever you go, whatever activity you're involved in, the work will be with you.

I well remember an evening, after a day of writing on *Careless Whispers*, when I was on a mind-clearing walk in the neighborhood.

I said hello to those I passed, petted the heads of a few friendly dogs, and was enjoying the twilight breeze when a sobering thought hit as if a tree had fallen. By then I was halfway through with the book and it was going well, but at that moment a chilling notion arrived.

What if something were to happen that would prevent my finishing it? I felt by then that I knew the complete story, its subtleties and nuances, better than even those who had lived it. It had become my sole responsibility to tell it, and I felt a sudden urge to quickly return home and get back to work. Such is the effect a writer can expect to experience as he marries himself to what becomes a mission.

When you reach that point—and you will if you strongly believe in what you're attempting to accomplish—embrace it, don't fight it. It's a sure sign that you're giving it your all.

Interviewing

YOU MAY BE THE MOST GIFTED wordsmith on Earth, but if your choice of expression is nonfiction, regardless of the topic, the successful interview is your professional bread and butter. If people aren't willing to answer your questions, confide their secrets, or explain their deepest thoughts, you best try becoming a poet. And good luck paying Junior's tuition with that.

While all are essential to the fact-finding process, interviews vary in degrees of importance. For a personality profile, of course, you need insightful, colorful anecdotes told by your subject and others who know him or her. In other cases, the interview is your best (and often only) way to get certain information your readers will want in your narrative.

I have never felt guilty or self-conscious about explaining to a subject that I know little or nothing about his profession or his area of expertise. I admit, right up front, that I will have some pretty dumb and elementary questions and hope he or she will be patient and kind enough to educate me. It has been my experience that deep down everyone loves being the teacher. Take advantage of it and you'll leave with the knowledge to convince your reader you might actually know what you're writing about.

I hate when I have to ask a potential interviewee, usually some important big shot, for "ten minutes," knowing their schedule is brim full and they'd rather visit the dentist than speak with a complete stranger writing for a publication they've never heard of. At such times, you can only be prepared to quickly ask the most important questions on your list. Ten minutes beats nothing, right? And, okay, truth is there are instances when your subject's time is every bit as valuable as yours.

In a perfect world, my interviews would all be conducted in a leisurely, conversational style. Before they were done I would know my subject, and my subject would have become involved enough to even learn a few things about me. It's called getting acquainted.

It doesn't happen that often, regardless of the topic you wish to discuss. Over the years, I've found that getting the tough interview often turns into a game. I'm not talking about the person who has said no to doing an interview. I mentioned earlier that I can appreciate and honor that.

But if the difficulty is getting close enough to even ask, it's another challenge altogether.

Years ago, veteran actor Ben Johnson was filming *The Sugarland Express* in Texas after having recently won an Academy Award for his brilliant performance as Sam the Lion in *The Last Picture Show*. I'd admired his work since his portrayal of one of the bad guys in *Shane* and suggested to the editor of the *Dallas Morning News* Sunday magazine that he was in the neighborhood and was one of the few showbiz personalities people didn't know that much about.

Given a green light to pursue a story, I placed a call to the on-set publicist to request an interview. I was politely informed that Johnson was on an extremely tight shooting schedule and finding time for me might be about as difficult as turning water to wine. But she said she would see what she could do and get back to me. I waited for her call which never came, then rang her back. Still working on it, she said, but don't get your hopes up. After about the third try over a period of a couple of weeks, I decided on a new approach.

I knew they would be filming in a rural area near San Antonio. "Here's what I'm going to do," I said. "I'll be there tomorrow morning and will just hang around until Mr. Johnson has time for either the interview or to personally tell me to get lost. Fair enough?"

The following day, she repeatedly reminded me of my time limit as we walked together toward Johnson's trailer.

He appeared at the door, we shook hands, and he invited me to join him on a nearby tree-shaded bench. Couldn't have been more hospitable. Yet the publicist stood impatiently by, arms folded, and not looking so happy. I can't say for certain, but she might have had a stopwatch in her pocket.

Explaining that I was fully aware that his time was limited, I went straight to a question I felt he might not have been asked of him since Oscar night. How, I wanted to know, did winning the Academy Award compare with the time he and his father had captured the World Team Roping title years earlier?

I had him. His eyes lit up. Soon he was talking about growing up days in Pawhuska, Oklahoma, of traveling to California as a teenager to wrangle a herd of horses his father had sold to motion picture icon John Ford, and how his roping skills, not acting talent, earned him his first lead role in *Mighty Joe Young*. My fifteen minutes expired, and the publicist rolled her pretty eyes and walked away.

Johnson and I talked until the caterers called for lunch. He invited me to join him so he could introduce me to the movie's young director, Stephen Spielberg. While we ate barbecue picnic style, he volunteered several thoughtful quotes.

As I began to worry that I'd l overstayed my welcome, Johnson waved off the notion and pointed out that the only scene he had to shoot that day was one with him sitting in an idle patrol car. He would have no lines. "Just get in the car," he said, "and when they're ready to shoot, you can duck down for a minute."

And so my fifteen minutes evolved into a full day, making my job far easier—and the story ever so much better.

By the way, Johnson told me his Oscar and that Team Roping trophy awarded to him and his dad sat side by side on his mantel.

The toolbox for interviewing is small and lightweight. A handheld recorder, a notebook, and pen or pencil. Even more important is to arrive with at least a few key questions in mind. Be wary of those which can be answered in a word or short sentence.

Years ago, I was waiting near the finishing hole of the Odessa Pro-Am to talk with PGA legend Don January. Standing beside me was a nervous young intern from the local paper. As we exchanged pleasantries, I learned that he had been assigned to interview January as well. On a legal pad, he had written out a half dozen questions, leaving empty lines below each to fill in his answers.

When January completed his round, he approached us, and I told my young fellow journalist that since he was likely on a tight deadline, he should ask his questions first. He did so, quickly running through his prepared list. The process took no more than about five minutes, and I could see cold panic in his eyes as realization set in. He simply didn't have enough material for a full-length story.

It was at that point that I watched a wonderful thing take place. Realizing the young man's dilemma, January began to ad lib, describing his round, praising the town's hospitality, and telling a funny anecdote or two while the relieved reporter wrote furiously.

By the time January finished, he had given the young reporter an excellent interview.

And I instantly became a fan. A class individual, he was aware the inexperienced reporter had a job to do and voluntarily took a few extra minutes to help him get it done.

It is important to put your subject at ease. I had just begun my series of interviews with Alvin, Texas, detective Sue Dietrick for *To the Last Breath*, and while she was extremely forthcoming, she hadn't completely made up her mind about my intentions. We'd met for a quick dinner, then I suggested that the privacy of my motel room might be the best place to talk. I didn't pick up on her hesitancy until she suggested it would be a good idea if we left the door open during the interview. I understood her concern.

At some point, my wife called to say a quick goodnight. I described the scene to her, even noting that I was keeping one foot on the motel room floor at all times. Overhearing my conversation from across the room, Detective Dietrick laughed. Thereafter, she was comfortable.

The interview went well, and I had learned another valuable lesson. Whenever possible, let the person you're interviewing pick the location.

If the world were populated by more Don Januarys, Ben Johnsons, and Sue Dietrichs, it would be a much better place, and a journalist's task would be far easier.

Where Story Ideas Come From

———

EXCEPT FOR SEEKING DETAILS about his or her income, the most asked question a writer will hear is where he or she gets ideas. It is always pretty clear that the person asking assumes there is some secret formula involved.

The fact is, it bears no resemblance to rocket science.

The ideas for your next project come two ways. Some editor, puffing his pipe while seated comfortably at his desk, has determined an urgent need for someone to trudge through hot, trash-strewn back alleys and tell the world what the daily life of a meter reader (remember him?) is really like. Others, fortunately, are move inventive, and their assignments offer more substance. Regardless, they are your friend and the guy who eventually instructs the paymaster to cut you a check. Without them, it's tough to stay in business.

I recall once visiting a well-regarded magazine editor's office, and when he excused himself for a bathroom break, I peeked at the handwritten list of story ideas he'd left on his desk. I didn't see a single one that remotely spurred my interest and privately dreaded the notion that since I had no brilliant idea of my own at the moment, I would shortly be leaving with one from his dreary list.

Given my druthers, I prefer those ideas I've come up with. In a sense, that makes them mine from the get-go since I wouldn't have bothered pitching them if they hadn't first caught my interest. And if one will look and listen carefully, the ideas are everywhere. To wit:

One day, while wandering Texas backroads, I came upon a weather-beaten "city limits" sign unfamiliar to me. Pelham, Texas, had a church, the remnants of an old school, a cemetery, and, I later learned, something less than forty residents. Curious, I began asking questions and was told that it was the last remaining all-Black town in the state. When enslaved people had been freed, local landowners had gifted each worker two hundred acres of farmland. And, as cotton crops prospered, the community grew to a population of over two hundred, had a busy general store, post office, school, and even formed its own amateur baseball team. I had literally driven onto a remarkable untold piece of Texas history.

Since at the time I was under contract to write a twice-monthly column for American Airlines's in-flight magazine, I quickly informed my editor of what my next subject would be. He liked the idea. So, ultimately, did the North American Travel Journalist Association which presented the column an award along with *Travel + Leisure* and *National Geographic*. Suddenly, and quite by accident, the folks of Pelham and I found ourselves in pretty fast company.

On another occasion, I was sitting in a Houston airport, reading the local paper while waiting to board my flight home. Buried in the sports section was a one-paragraph story announcing that Asherton High School's basketball team had finally won a game after years of losing. The last sentence noted that the tiny school's football team currently owned the national high school losing streak record.

Since fall was fast approaching, I had two things I needed to do quickly. First, I had to find out where in hell Asherton was, then I needed to call a friendly editor at *Parade* magazine, the Sunday insert of hundreds of US newspapers, and convince him to let me do the story before the new season opened.

Given the go-ahead, I found the small migrant worker community deep in South Texas. There was but one paved road in the town, and the football coach had earned his position only because no one else wanted the job. Many of his players were still working the fields up north with their families and wouldn't make it home until school got underway. Uniforms were old and badly in need of repair. A giant ant bed sprawled at midfield in the downtrodden stadium. No player in the past decade had received a letter jacket for the simple reason there was no room for them in the budget.

But they were determined to play, and the community supported them. After all, it was Texas, where high school football ranks right up there with Sunday-go-to-meeting. Thus, the story I wrote was not about a hapless group of untalented kids and their clueless coach but of a group of young people butting heads against incredible odds.

The response to "The Team That Never Wins" was incredible. Donations from readers began arriving in the school mailbox. A syndicated radio host called to ask that each Friday night score be phoned in to him so he could be the first to spread the word about the Trojans' first victory. Inmates of a Georgia prison adopted Asherton High as "their team." Sisters in an out-of-state convent promised to keep them in their prayers. And the Houston Oilers sent a truckload of equipment.

As a writer, there is no greater reward than realizing a positive response to what one's written.

And it all happened because of one short sentence in a newspaper. Yes, the written word can be a powerful thing.

Even a book can develop from such serendipity.

Years ago, against my better judgment, I agreed to a short camping trip in the vast Big Bend region of Texas. If you love thorny cactus and sand and blistering temperatures, it is the ideal vacation spot. For one who prefers sleeping indoors under the gentle hum of an air conditioner, not so much.

One early morning, near the welcomed end of our trip, we were planning a visit to see some abandoned felspar mines when our route took us through the tiny way-stop of Study Butte. Off in the distance, just beyond a tiny post office, was a small, well-kept adobe building. "That's the school," my more experienced friend said. "One room, one teacher."

I had to meet this guy.

By the time I'd had coffee with Trent Jones, learning how he and his wife had fallen in love with the isolated region, had wanted out of the big city rat race, and had made their adventurous move to the middle of nowhere, I was wishing I had my notebook. He explained that he was superintendent, principal, custodian, and teacher of grades 1–7, earning a pauper's $4,500 per annum. His twenty-one students arrived daily from ranches as far as fifty miles away.

At the time we met, he had learned that the Texas Education Agency was demanding that his tiny school meet accreditation guidelines. Though none of his students were disabled, he'd seen to it that his one-story building was wheelchair accessible. Also on the lengthy list of demands was a fully stocked school library. With only textbooks and limited space, he had located an abandoned mobile home which he talked a couple of ranchers into hauling to the side of his school. Then, wife Olga launched a letter-writing campaign to friends and librarians across the state, asking for any books they were planning to discard. Voila, instant library and another checked box on the to-do list.

Jones ultimately received notification that his school would be fully accredited.

I told his story to the readers of *People* magazine. Soon after its publication, a call came from an editor at Playboy Press, of all places, asking if Jones might be interested in telling a lengthier version of his fascinating story. And, if so, would I like to help him with it? He didn't even ask me to write a proposal.

Trent and his wife, Olga, embraced the idea (and the notion of added income), and we agreed on a coauthor partnership that resulted in *Where the Rainbows Wait.* The title came from an old cowboy's description of the arid region as a place "where the rainbows wait for rain."

We didn't make any bestseller lists, but Jones's heroic story earned him applause from readers and high praise from reviewers. The sales department at Playboy Press was reasonably happy. One of the network morning shows dispatched a crew to film a piece on the teacher and his little one-room school. When it aired, it was necessary for Jones and his kids to make a forty-mile day trip to find the nearest television set.

And, yes, there was a movie option that generated brief excitement among the children until it became clear nothing was going to happen.

Originally published in 1978, the book, still one of my favorites, has lived through several reprint publishers, most recently one called Iron Mountain Press. By the time that offer came, Trent and Olga had taken their leave, feeling a need for a more well-rounded environment for their young daughters, Cassandra and Maria. They'd moved to California. But a piece of Jones's heart remained in his one-room school.

It was his idea that we donate any royalty earnings to help fund the building of an outdoor basketball court for the school. He announced the plan, which I wholeheartedly supported, at a reunion gathering of his former students.

I was honored that I was invited to attend.

As time passes, you'll learn more tricks of the trade. They'll usually come just after the hot water heater has blown up or when you have a throbbing toothache and no dental insurance. If the piper is to be paid, the writer must produce.

One of the most impressive ways of expanding freelance earnings I learned came from a fellow newsman who supplemented his income by writing short news items for a variety of trade publications. The pay was minuscule, but the work amounted to only a few minutes on the phone and a half hour at his computer.

He would then recycle like crazy. After hitting on a saleable idea, he would write it, rewrite it, then rewrite it again. Sometimes he'd compose a half dozen versions of the same article, determining which markets weren't in direct competition, and start mailing. In time, he would collect an impressive stack of twenty-five to fifty-dollar checks. I think his one-story-recycle record was twelve.

It all adds up.

I'll not bore you with the number of times I've sold basically the same story several times. Here, however, is one example.

In Hye, Texas, I had learned that back during the Depression a family of nine bothers had made up the starting lineup of its town baseball team. Not only were several of the Deike brothers still living and thus available for interviews, but adding to the fascinating story was the fact a teenage neighbor named Lyndon B. Johnson had occasionally driven over on Sunday afternoons to play first base.

It was my kind of story. I first sold it to *Sports Illustrated*. Later, I expanded it into a cover story for the Sunday magazine of the *Houston Chronicle*. Then, I developed it into a small book titled *Oh Brother, How They Played the Game* for State House Press.

It traveled well.

Style

___

THIS IS ANOTHER OF THE writing elements that has long puzzled me. I have friends and readers who swear they can recognize something I've written, even if it carries no byline or my name on the dustjacket. I'm not sure they're being honest or just flattering the old codger.

There was never a time when I consciously sat down and told myself, okay, today's the day I'm going to develop a style of writing. While in college I did write one hundred or so pages of a would-be novel that so badly mimicked J. D. Salinger's *Catcher in the Rye* it was absolutely embarrassing. Fortunately, no one read it before I wisely tossed it.

So, what exactly is "style"?

Is it Hemingway and his bare-bone sentences? Faulkner, who could never find the end of a sentence? The Beat generation writer who refused the use of capital letters or punctuation, as if his keyboard wasn't functioning properly? Could it be that some who point to "their style" are just using a literary gimmick to draw attention?

Even the world's most famous hermit, Salinger, stubbed his toe on dialogue occasionally, in my humble opinion. Why have his little buddy Holden Caulfield ask, "Jeetjet?" when he could just as easily have had him say, "Have you eaten yet?"

A few years ago, writer Glenn Dromgoole and I were asked to coauthor an ambitious undertaking that would be titled *101 Essential Texas Books*. And, while I felt our picks were first rate, not one was selected because of the author's writing style. We simply compiled a list and wrote short reviews of a dandy collection of works that were informative, entertaining, valuable to society, and, yes, quite well written.

All that said, I should note that my wife is proof positive that certain writing styles do exist.

We were visiting a bookstore, and she was exercising her usual routine of scanning a few pages of any novel that caught her interest. She called me over, showed me a book by an unknown writer named Richard Bachman.

"This," she commented, "reads very much like a Stephen King novel." It was months before someone blew the horror master's cover and revealed that he'd been writing books under the Bachman pseudonym for some time. Pat had discovered his secret—and, yes, his style—in just those few pages.

If a gun was put to my head, I'd define the way I write as something closely kin to the way I talk, removing the "ughs" and cussing and repetitions, of course. No big words when smaller ones get the job done, no rambling sentences with a half dozen subjects stirred in. I try to keep things simple, conversational, and fast-paced. If I'm able to hold the reader's interest, I've done my job.

Nothing fancy. Over the years, it has become what I'm comfortable with.

I've never been accused of flaunting my vocabulary or attempting to knock the reader off his or her feet with ultraflowery descriptions of glowing sunsets and green meadows. It was another pretty good writer, Elmore Leonard, who had a rule he stuck to when editing his own work: take out all the words that sound like writing. Advice to live by.

But, conceding there is a writing style, it is developed slowly and with little notice. An editor's red pencil might have helped show the way. Maybe even a lecture heard at a writer's gathering. You may have begun to hear it when reading something you've written aloud. And don't tell anybody, but in your leisure reading you might have subconsciously borrowed a technique or two from someone who has already mastered the craft.

You're only asking for trouble should you attempt to blatantly imitate some guy or gal sitting atop the *Times* Best Seller list. I've been a fan of the legendary John Steinbeck's lyrical prose all my adult life but would be an absolute fool to think I could ever write like him. It would embarrass me and cause him to roll over in his grave.

I keep repeating myself, but it all comes down to determine the best way to tell your story. Storytelling. Some are good at it; some barely pass muster. A few will put you in coma.

So, having determined there is, in fact, such a thing as an individual writing style, what are the rules we should follow? Beyond putting words together in a way you feel comfortable with (there's that word again) and think your reader will enjoy, there really aren't many.

If you're dead set on ignoring grammar and punctuation and writing sentences that run on for pages, have at it and best of luck. Just don't expect me to be among your loyal readers.

While it may not fit into the fine definition of style, developing the ability to describe places and people lends greatly to both fiction and nonfiction. The reader wants to know what your hero or villain looks like, from hair color to the clothes they wear and any unusual mannerisms they might have. Picture your subjects/characters in your mind's eye. Does he scowl or smile, limp or take long, gliding strides? Is he always popping his knuckles or running his fingers through his hair? Tall, short, muscular? Does he have a unique speech pattern?

In providing these details, you have invented a plausible character your reader can see.

This is among those tools that are of great value but, in my opinion, often overused. One of my favorite mystery writers must be something of a clothes horse since he delights in describing every item of clothing his characters wear. He even provides brand names. For my taste, that's too much information.

With nonfiction, of course, all one need do is be keenly aware of how one's subject looks, acts, and dresses, then pass a good description along to the reader.

The satisfied reader will also have been provided a strong sense of place.

When John and Jane are in a park, discussing where they'll go for dinner, the reader needs to be sitting on the bench with them. Describe the flowers blooming nearby, the squirrels chasing around, the rolling black thunderclouds forming in the distance, the sun turning into a giant orange ball as it sets.

Again, with nonfiction your job will have been done for you. If, during an interview, John tells you about that decision-making conversation with Jane, ask him to recall the locale. He can tell you about the passing lady having a conversation with her poodle or remember the scent of the nearby moss roses or how the breeze tossed Jane's hair.

Setting such a scene adds another layer in your effort to bring your reader into the story.

Finally, for a far more learned discussion of the matter, I heartedly suggest reading *The Elements of Style* by William Strunk and E. B. White. Less than one hundred pages in length, it is the time-tested final say on the subject. I yield to the masters.

Editors: Friend or Foe

————

YOUR EDITOR, like the guy from IRS, is always right. Deal with it.

As soon as you release your manuscript to his or her care, it is no longer your sole property. You've sold your rights (and some say your soul) not only to the publisher but an editor. They will make changes, suggest revisions, question why you used a certain word or phrase, and sometimes make you feel the principal has decided to demote you a grade or two.

They do these things because they're the best friend a writer has.

Without an editor's keen eye, every mistake, clunky phrase, mis-spelling, and tense boo-boo you've committed would make it into the public plaza. Their job is to make your writing better and save you all manner of embarrassment.

As with any profession, naturally, there are those who are good at their jobs and some who obviously got their position because they're the boss's no-talent son-in-law. But it has been my experience that most are not only sharp but have a deep and abiding love for the language.

It is at their doorstep that you want to put your ego in check. Not every one of the 100,000 words in your book is as precious as you might think. Some of your hilarious anecdotes ain't really that funny and need to go. And that working title you just love? Forget it; they'll come up with a better one (with suggestions from brains over in the sales and marketing department).

The writer who isn't willing to admit his imperfections and accept an editor's help is only making unneeded problems for himself.

Back in my newspaper days, I saw egos so big they wouldn't fit into the Astrodome. Talented writers, who had heard positive feedback from adoring fans and had probably won an obscure writing prize or two, viewed every word they wrote as sacred, not to be touched, changed, or frowned upon by an editor. Just slap a catchy headline on it and send it along to the typesetter.

Instead of occupying a low rung on the publishing pecking order, editors are your guardian angel. You would do well to buy them an occasional beer or send a thank-you note every now and then. Not only do they have the power and the upper hand but can make your life miserable if you're inclined to start a fight.

Still, the professionals will welcome a constructive conversation about wording or tone or turn of phrase that might even find you the winner. But if you're determined to argue for argument's sake—talk down to them—buddy, you're in for a long day.

My experience with editors has been overwhelmingly rewarding. My articles and books have been improved by their interest and involvement. They'll get little, if any, public acknowledgment, but their tireless suggestions and improvements can make or break careers. They're who will quietly discover the unknowns and nurture them to success.

When my dear editor Freddie Goff accompanied us to New York to accept the Edgar, she got not one clap of applause, nor was she asked for a sound bite or had her picture taken. She received no duplicate of the coveted prize and, so far as I know, got no appreciative bonus from her employer. I don't even remember a glass being raised to her. I knew, however, how much she had contributed to making *Careless Whispers* as good as possible and how invested she had become in the project, so I wanted to somehow show my appreciation. I wouldn't have been there, decked out in my Sunday finest, without her.

The morning following the awards dinner, I visited a jewelry store near Radio City Music Hall and, with my wife's help, picked out a small, gold apple (signifying our successful visit to the Big Apple, natch) that dangled from a delicate chain. My editor has worn it proudly since.

Small thanks, but a heartfelt reminder.

Bear this in mind the next time you submit a manuscript: in today's cutback, downsizing work environment, the editor on whose desk your article or book lands probably has a half dozen or more other projects in progress. Still, they'll patiently double-check some obscure fact for you, make sure everyone's name is correctly spelled, and get all the dates right. Grunge work, but a necessary part of the job.

And, for God's sake, don't pull an F. Scott Fitzgerald.

As the story goes, his weary editor phoned him one day to say she had looked through every dictionary in the building yet was unable to check the spelling or learn the meaning of a certain word he'd written. Fitzgerald asked what the word was, and when told, explained that it wasn't actually a word, just a sound he'd come up with. "Just read the sentence and see how beautifully it makes it flow," he explained. I can only guess that he must have been drinking at the time.

Having now praised Caesar, I should admit to the occasional moments of frustration.

There was a small regional magazine I'd contributed to for years without any writer-editor hostilities. I sent in an assigned story, satisfied I'd done a relatively good job. What came back to me after a week or so was a version that was various shades of awful. It had been completely rewritten. I blew my top and was ready for a full-out shouting match when I called my editor to suggest we just forget the whole thing. I didn't want my name on such an immature version of my story. She could find something else to keep the ads from bumping into one another.

She laughed, then explained. They had just hired a young summer intern who they'd given my article to edit as a test exercise. "Maybe he tried a little too hard," the editor said, "and he wasn't supposed to have sent you his edit. I'll send mine in a few days."

All ended well.

On another occasion, after ghostwriting a book for a celebrated motivational speaker, she was mortified when the edited manuscript returned. How, she wanted to know, could there have been so many mistakes and needs for change on almost every page? She didn't come right out with it, but it was clear she felt I'd not done my best.

She simply had no understanding of the publishing world.

In truth, the editing was modest, about what I had expected. By the time her book was published, she couldn't have been happier.

It is important to understand that every editor won't share your enthusiasm for the story you've proposed. Pardon the cliches when I say stick to your guns and go to war with your best ammunition. If it still doesn't fly, there's always another publication to try.

There was a time when I attended story meetings in the offices of the *Dallas Observer*, one of those free alternative weeklies that exist to publish sexy ads for gentlemen's clubs and massage parlors. That, as I've mentioned earlier, is where I pitched my idea of visiting a rural community to write about its six-man football team.

Had the editor, whose interests ran from political scandal to more political scandal, not been in dire need of stories, she probably would never have given me the green light. A further sign of her lack of any genuine interest came later when the piece I wrote on little Penelope was given no consideration for the upcoming week's cover.

Ah, but a few months later, it was the editor's duty to inform me she'd just been notified that the article had been selected to appear in the annual *Best American Sports Writing* anthology along with pieces from publications like *Sports Illustrated*, the *New York Times*, and *The New Yorker*. I politely thanked her and silently declared myself the winner—even before I got a contract to expand the story into *Where Dreams Die Hard*.

Finally, I would be remiss if I didn't mention the time a *People* editor got me fired.

The magazine was working on a story of Ted Kaczynski, the manifesto-writing Unabomber, and somehow learned that his whistleblowing brother, David, had briefly lived in a self-made dugout far out in the Big Bend region (the same area where I first met schoolteacher Trent Jones). Supposedly, Ted had once visited there.

As quickly as possible, they wanted everything I could piece together. I said I'd be on my way immediately but was told there wasn't time for me to make the six-hundred-mile trip. Just do the best you can on the phone, I was instructed.

I went to work, locating a few people who remember the brother, a relative of the deceased rancher who had owned the land on which the strange living quarters were located, and I was putting together a description of the desert locale from memory when *People's* photo editor called.

"We've got a photographer in the air, on his way," he breathlessly said, "and I need the exact location of this dugout. Now."

I told him I didn't have a clue, then came the explosion. He roared at me, asking what in hell I was doing out there. Telling him I wasn't "there" didn't register. He just yelled louder. The plane carrying the photographer was scheduled to be there in an hour. I reminded him it had been his magazine's decision for me not to do on-site reporting. His yelling turned a dark shade of blue as he said he would see to it that I'd worked my last story for *People* magazine.

I took it as a challenge. After several more calls, I learned that the only local who had ever visited brother Kaczynski's underground vacation home no longer lived in the Big Bend. He'd moved to a small town near San Antonio where he was a high school teacher.

I phoned the school and, doing my best to convince a bewildered secretary that it was a life-and-death matter, persuaded her to call the teacher from his classroom. He came to the phone and provided directions as I furiously took notes.

Then I called the still-irate photo editor.

Here, I told him, are your directions: "Follow the Interstate south out of Terlingua for ten miles . . . then turn left onto the only Farm to Market road in the area . . . Go about five miles until you pass a big, white two-story . . . Just beyond it there will be a barbed wire fence and a gate and cattle guard. Go through it and after about five more miles and there'll be a fork in the road . . . Turn right . . . then start looking for a stand of mesquite trees off near a small sandhill. That's where your damn picture will be."

I'm ashamed to say, but I think I recall slamming down the phone.

I never heard from the photo editor again but did get a call a few days later from an apologetic bureau chief who had made the original assignment. All's well, she said, you're still our Dallas correspondent.

And in the next week's issue, there, alongside the Kaczynski story, was a photograph of the dugout. The world continued to spin.

While on the subject of photographers and direction seeking, I should include this final anecdote:

A cameraman from the Big Apple was in Fort Worth to help chronicle a gruesome murder and needed directions to a countryside location where the crime had occurred. Again, it was one of those

Texas-style instructions—winding two-lane roads, various landmarks, barbed wire fences, and a cattle guard near where the body had been found.

For those of you who don't know, a cattle guard is a row of closely spaced pipes cemented into the ground at the pasture gate. It prevents the livestock from escaping. Every old rancher knows what I'm talking about. But, obviously, not out-of-state journalists.

After receiving his directions, the visitor had but one question. "What kind of uniform," he wanted to know, "will the cattle guard be wearing?" New Yorkers, you've got to love them.

But I digress.

If, somewhere out there, there's a major magazine piece or book worth reading that has gone straight from writer to publication without the input of a keen-eyed editor, I'd love to know about it, then will vigorously shake the author's hand.

That said, I'll close this discussion since I'm expecting a call from an editor working on a profile I've written about a man whose hobby it has been to run at least a mile in each of Texas's 254 counties. Hey, whatever floats your boat and makes for a good read.

Literary Agents

THE FIRST THING of any consequence I ever managed to sell was a lengthy piece I submitted to *Sports Illustrated.* An innocent in the writing business at the time, I mailed off the story on a Texas high school football dynasty to Tex Maule, one of the magazine's legendary staff writers. I included a note, recalling our having briefly met in some press box, and asked how much trouble it would be to route my story to the proper editor's desk.

Next thing I knew, my article was sold and a big shot *SI* photographer would soon be on his way to illustrate it

See how easy it was?

Same with an over-the-transom submission I made to *TV Guide* back in the days when *Bonanza* was still part of the prime-time line-up. I visited actor Dan Blocker's panhandle hometown of O'Donnell, Texas, wrote about his growing up days, licked a few stamps, and blindly mailed it off. Next thing I knew it was a cover story for the largest circulation magazine in the country at the time.

Man, those were the days. Now gone.

Today, even the major magazines hold fast to a rule that they will only consider submissions from established literary agents. Book publishers as well. I'm not certain what caused this new layer of protection for editorial offices. Maybe nothing more than a landslide of too much time-wasting, badly written prose showing up in the mailroom.

Who are these literary agents and what is their purpose? The quick answer in today's publishing world is that they are essential. They are your doorway to the publisher's office, the person who states your case, makes certain the contract agreement you're about to sign is fair, serves as the pipeline between you and your editor, and potentally gives your manuscript a quick edit before shipping it off. Your agent is a well-versed detail person with an ear for everything from double negatives to a catchy title and an eye for what makes the book jacket work. The agent will fight the fights you want to avoid and might even lend a sympathetic ear if you catch him on a good day. The agent will steer you away from bad ideas and, if necessary, force-feed you good ones.

Where, then, does the aspiring writer find such a person? It's the question that leads us head-on into the old chicken-or-egg discussion. Agents are everywhere and nowhere.

Literary agents, who earn their 12.5–15 percent of any contract they successfully negotiate for you, are constantly in search of experienced writers to represent. Meanwhile, the beginning writer, who has no portfolio, needs an experienced agent. Round peg, square hole. How to make them fit?

Agents aren't hard to find. It is just difficult to convince them that you can be a moneymaker for them. They're listed on rosters in virtually all publications related to publishing and marketing. Most even have their own websites. But cold calls aren't likely to get their attention when they come in the middle of negotiations for a three-book deal for someone who's been with them for a decade.

What you do is scramble, ask around, and say a little prayer before bedtime. You ask other writers if their agent is taking on new clients. If one agent turns you down, ask if there is someone he or she might recommend. When you find someone who looks promising, learn what kind of books they're looking for. There's little use signing on with an agent who specializes in Chinese cookbooks and coffee table prehistoric art hardbacks when what you want to write (and sell) are heart-pounding mysteries or a Civil War history.

If you can get your foot in the door with the agent who seems right for you, be sure you make a good first impression. There will be a time in your career when the idea of doing a full-length or mostly finished manuscript before pitching it becomes absurdity, but if you can show him or her your completed book or at least the first hundred pages or so with a detailed outline, you've taken a first big step. First, you have immediately proven yourself to be one who can go the distance.

Second, if he or she likes what they read, and they think some of their editorial contacts might, there's a good chance you can walk away with a new agent.

And who of us doesn't like being the center of attention at a cocktail party, saying, "Well, according to my agent . . ."?

If all goes according to plan, you'll have written your last complete book without a contract serving as a safety net.

That said, the requirements of agents vary. For fiction, they will need a generous sample of your book (maybe one hundred pages), while for nonfiction, a thorough proposal and maybe a sample chapter or two should get the job done. Such are the guidelines the two of you will work out.

Writers Beware! If you run across an "agent" named Swifty who will read and critique your manuscript for the low, low price of $500, turn and run.

When you have found someone who might fit your needs and seems genuinely interested in you, don't be shy about asking questions. What are some of the titles he or she has recently sold? What publishing houses does the agent have a long-term relationship with? Are they interested in the genre you wish to work in, and do they know specific editors who like the same kind of fantasy or police procedural you do?

From that day you reach an agreement, the literary agent becomes your business manager. When you propose a new book idea, it is his or her's first duty to give you a candid opinion. Nope, there's just no way to persuade a New York editor to shell out good money for a sprawling novel based on Grandpa's old cotton farming ledgers or collecting Buffalo nickels for fun and profit. But, yes, the agent knows a couple of friendly editors who are always looking for a science fiction novel with some new twist, or a World War II battle on which you've dug up new information.

You listen to him or her to learn new trends, what's hot, what's not. If you're not looking for guidance, don't waste the agent's or your time.

While agents I've met like to refer to themselves as generalists, most do have areas of special interest. It goes with the territory.

Larger agencies, with several agents on staff, will divide the specialties among themselves. For now, however, we are talking about the lone agent sitting in his cluttered office, puffing on his pipe while searching frantically for the next Tom Clancey or Sandra Brown.

Now that you've signed up and sent off your manuscript, respect your agent's time. Believe it or not, you aren't the only person they're working for. You haven't contracted for a best friend, just a knowledgeable guide to the publishing doorway.

Your agent will keep you posted if there's something newsworthy to pass along while educating you in the glacial nature of the publishing business.

When you do get your agent on the phone, listen carefully to what's being said. Tweak that proposal, rewrite that opening chapter, consider expanding a certain character. You're paying for advice. Take it.

I've known writers who routinely fire their agents, bemoaning the fact they haven't succeeded in making enough sales or stayed in touch as often as the client would like. While some partnerships just don't work, I wonder if it is sometimes easier to lay blame at the agent's feet instead of taking a hard look in the mirror. Instead of constantly looking for a new representative, time might be better spent finishing the book you promised a year and a half ago.

Give the agent something to work with and he or she will become your champion. Your agent will have no reservation about calling up a particular reviewer or TV producer to suggest they should pay more attention to your latest work. The agent will be on the lookout for speaking opportunities, a guest spot needing to be filled at a book festival, and they'll make sure your publisher has offered foreign rights to countries you've never heard of. In most instances, it will be your agent who the movie people first reach out to with their pie-in-the-sky offers.

Personally, I've been lucky. Janet Manus was two things that I needed when I was searching for an agent. She was highly respected in New York publishing circles and was a fan of true crime books. We got in touch following the publication of *Careless Whispers*, had dinner one evening at a Manhattan bistro, and had made a deal before the check came. Part mother hen, part pit bull, she would be my guiding light for over a decade.

After her passing, longtime friend Jim Donovan, who I had watched carve himself a place as a respected literary agent, offered to fill the void. When he found a home for my wayward *Where Dreams Die Hard* and pointed me toward fiction, I knew I'd drawn to an inside straight a second time.

You should be so lucky.

Now, I had every intention of closing this section with a few funny stories about literary agents. But there are no funny stories about literary agents.

Voices: Yours and Theirs

DESPITE THE FACT the book now in your hands is overloaded with "I's" and "me's" and various other first-person references, it is not my favored brand of writing. Give me a good third-person narrative and a cup of hot coffee, and I'm happy.

That admission made, it should be noted that the more comfortable you are in a variety of idioms, the better off you'll be.

Most of my writing, even my western fiction, has been done from a third-person viewpoint. I prefer telling the story without putting myself into it, letting the subject say what he has to say without bothering to mention he said it to me. It's often been said that the best football refereeing and baseball umpiring comes when the participants and fans don't notice the officials are involved. A good writer is much the same.

Pulitzer Prize–winning sportswriter Red Smith once explained to me that while writing his column, he always felt he was simply "driving the getaway car."

But, as always, we have exceptions to the rules. Like when writing this little book of suggestions. Or a column wherein you're sharing your thoughts and feelings on a particular subject. Or writing an autobiography.

When I decided to write *Sins of the Son*—the book about my eldest boy's misspent life, his bad decisions, and eventual arrest and imprisonment for murder—it occurred to me there was no way I could treat it as I had previous true crime efforts. The story I had in mind was far different, too personal, my involvement too much a part of the journey. It would have been a cop-out had I tried to make myself and my parenting shortcomings invisible.

Placing myself in the story worked. No book I'd written before or since received such reader response. Moms and dads wrote to say that I had, in a manner of speaking, told the story of their own parental frustrations and that they had found some solace in knowing they weren't alone. A young woman, finally recovered from drug addition, tearfully called to say that after reading the book she had been in touch with her family for the first time in years.

Most important was my own new understanding that resulted from the project. Sitting in a prison visiting room or exercise yard, interviewing my grown son in the same manner I would any other subject, provided me an avenue to ask questions never before asked and, in return, hear honest answers for the first time.

Still, writing the book was more difficult than any I've ever attempted, for reasons that went far beyond writing in the first person.

Since then, I've inserted myself into my writing only when musing in an *American Way* column or an editorial page essay about a day at the ballpark in the company of my grandson, a twilight visit to my canine pals in the neighborhood, or bidding farewell to a well-known friend. I found that not only do I enjoy occasionally writing in the first person but that it can be the best way to tell the story. Yep, old dogs can learn new tricks.

If there is a trick to it, it lies in the ability to not go overboard with the personal references. It is not essential to constantly remind the reader that you're there, front and center, unless you're confessing to some high crime.

I well remember a time when it became a game to count the number of *I's* the columnist for a rival paper used in each of his columns. Avoid that trap at all costs.

A final plea: never, ever slip into that pompous vernacular wherein you refer to yourself as "this writer." I prefer the sound of fingernails scratching along the surface of a blackboard.

Few journalists I know haven't secretly wished to write a column. Not one on oil and gas prices or the ongoing hazards of global warming, but what is called a "general column." Tightly written in seven hundred well-considered words or so, it is journalism's most personal art form, as close to a free rein as you're going to get. Its writer has freedom to choose his topic and pick his approach while on the way to becoming the next Rick Bragg or Dave Barry. He can be warm and fuzzy, funny, empathetic, or highly POed as he speaks directly to his reader.

I recall overhearing one writer tell a columnist friend, "For years, you've been telling your life story, seven hundred words at a time." It was a valid observation, given that his readers had developed a great fondness for his whimsical tales of family tribulations, his bragging on his grandson's election into the National Honor Society, and his charming nostalgic reflections.

Be aware that it isn't easy. Which brings to mind another great Red Smith one-liner. Once asked if column-writing was difficult, he replied, "No. All one need do is sit at the typewriter, open a blood vein, and start writing."

Back in my newspapering days, I was a hit-and-miss sports columnist. Okay on those days when I felt I had something worthwhile to say but a colossal bore when I did little but fill up space. During the time I did it regularly (and read fellow columnists), I came to quickly realize that it was a pursuit with a high rate of burnout. With rare exceptions, people eventually run out of something new to say. Those who can maintain a high quality over a long period of time have a special kind of genius on their side.

For me, it is a form of writing best taken in small doses.

For five years, I wrote a twice-monthly back-of-the-magazine column/essay for *American Way* magazine. It was the most enjoyable gig I've ever had, and I felt I gave them their money's worth. Reader feedback to my "Americana" was good, it won a few prizes, and the columns were even collected in a little book titled *On Texas Backroads*.

Publication of the little book provided another dilemma. Glenn Dromgoole, who seems always to be coming to my rescue, was aware that my wife wanted to see my columns in book form and offered to publish it under his little Texas Star Trading Company imprint. I worried that he was simply being generous and wasn't likely to get back his printing costs.

Slowly, but surely, to my relief, it edged toward the break-even point. Then, suddenly, Glenn announced that a second printing, even larger than the first, was being ordered. Our savior was the Mansfield

Reads! program, held annually by the local Friends of the Mansfield Public Library. Like many communities are now doing (bless them one and all), a single book would be selected, promoted, and suggested to every reader in town. They had selected *On Texas Backroads*, and the hoopla would all wrap up with a gala, Evening with the Author program.

Inside the city limits of Mansfield, Texas, I suddenly had a best-seller. They even graciously presented me the key to the city.

Publisher Dromgoole never did so in my presence, but I'm sure he gave out a quiet sigh of relief.

Yet, on that day when word came that American Airlines bean counters had decided to farm the publication out to an in-flight magazine group that saw no further need for what I wrote, I shed few tears.

Why not? At that moment, I hadn't the foggiest idea what the subject of my next column would be.

Ghostwriting

————

GHOSTWRITING OFFERS yet another first-person exercise that can be demanding. You are telling someone else's story, usually one about his or her life or professional experiences, and must constantly remind yourself that he or she is telling the story, not you. So, whether you're writing an entertainer's memoirs or busy helping a CEO explain how selling widgets can be fun and profitable, you must constantly remind yourself it is their book, not yours.

When NFL Hall of Fame running back Marcus Allen asked that I lend a hand with his autobiography, my first order of business was to get to know him. Initially, I was more interested in how he expressed himself than how many touchdowns he'd scored during his remarkable career. To do him a proper job, I needed to learn his speech patterns and rhythms, his favored expressions. I needed to be sure that *Marcus* would read like he was the author.

Only then did we proceed to the interviews that provided me his life story. And he eventually made the *New York Times* and *Los Angeles Times* bestseller lists.

The same procedure applied as I prepared to write *FBI Undercover* for Special Agent Larry Wansley and *Happy Trails* with Roy Rogers and Dale Evans.

Ghostwriting can be enjoyable or an absolute car crash. It is fun, frankly, to take on someone else's identity for a bit, reliving dramatic moments and historic events in which they participated. As a kid, I had cheered for Roy and his wonder horse Trigger when they rounded up the bad guys every Saturday afternoon during the Texas Theater matinee. (Admission nine cents for those of us twelve and under.) And as an adult, there I was, hired to play the role of my screen hero by proxy.

There was a bonus to that particular project.

During the time I was visiting with Rogers in Victorville, California, my previous wife's birthday was fast approaching. Inasmuch as she viewed the annual milestone as something akin to a national holiday, I knew I could expect a sizable amount of grief for missing the celebration.

I was sitting in Rogers's office, preparing for another day of interviews, when the big day arrived. My dark mood must have been obvious since Roy asked if I was feeling okay. I explained my problem.

"Get her on the phone," he said.

When she answered, I quickly handed the receiver to the King of the Cowboys and listened as he sang "Happy Birthday" to her. The only thing that could have made the moment better would have been for the Sons of the Pioneers to be harmonizing in the background.

Beat that, fellow shoppers.

Be forewarned that sometime in the collaborative process your subject, regardless of his training or profession, will decide he's become a writer. Instead of just offering helpful comments and suggestions to the manuscript you've written for him, he may start to insert paragraph or page here and there, changing phrases, deciding he can make a funny story even funnier. Tinkering, I call it.

After all, it is his book. But woe is me. Do your gentle best to urge him to leave well enough alone.

Some years back, a writer friend had enjoyed considerable success ghosting a series of true crime books for a big-city homicide detective. My friend confided to me some of the hair-pulling difficulties he'd experienced but admitted it was worth the headaches. The books were selling well.

In time, the cop-turned-writer was the subject of a glowing newspaper profile in which he described in agonizing detail the toils of the writing process. Though he admitted it was difficult work, he pointed out that he felt he had improved with each subsequent book and had learned to embrace his craft.

Not once did he admit that he'd never written a single word of any of the books or tip his hat to his ghostwriter.

My friend, a pro, just grinned and beared it. Perils of the trade, he said.

Writing Fiction

———

UNLIKE MANY in my circle of contemporaries, it was never a life's goal to write the Great American Novel. For me, fiction was something to read, not write. Oh, there was that aborted effort in my college days to invent my own Holden Caufield, but since then if I felt the urge it would quickly pass after I took a couple of aspirin and a short nap.

I was quite happy laboring in the nonfiction fields.

Then, my agent relayed a question posed by Tom Colgan, a Signet editor who oversaw a series of paperback westerns. A famed writer in the genre, Ralph Compton, had died, leaving behind a legion of devoted fans. To keep readers happy, Signet and Compton's heirs had reached an agreement to continue publishing westerns under the Compton brand, though they would, of course, be written by others. You had to look hard at the covers to see the fine print line that would read, A Ralph Compton Novel by So-and-So.

Apparently, it was working. And would I like to try my hand at writing one?

Truth is, I had never read a Ralph Compton novel. Nor, for that matter, many westerns. My basic experience in the genre had come from watching Dad race through one Louis L'Amour or Max Brand paperback after another and admiring the success of longtime friend and multiple Spur Award-winner Elmer Kelton.

So, naturally, I told Colgan that I'd love to write a western.

I assumed Compton had a John Wayne–like featured character who I would need to get to know and then attempt to portray in the originator's style. No, the editor said, each is a stand-alone book— your story, your characters, major and minor. There were, in fact, only a few guidelines. The novels needed to be 80,000 words in length and devoid of sex and foul language. Too, in order to maintain the hectic publishing schedule, I would have three months to get the book written. Obviously, Compton fans were fast readers.

To get us on our way, all Colgan needed was a brief synopsis of the novel I planned to write. Since he'd indicated I had leeway to plot and characters, I came up with a ne'er-do-well rancher's son as my protagonist. He would be getting out of jail after having been arrested for drunkenly busting up the town saloon. His sister would explain that their daddy hadn't returned from a trip.

That settled, I planned to insert a bit of historical fact. In the late 1800s, the diabolical Bender family had run a middle-of-nowhere way station in Kansas, offering weary travelers' food and lodging. In a carefully orchestrated manner, they would kill the visitor, rob him, and bury his body in their nearby orchard. Historians called them the Bloody Benders, and the daughter was generally believed to be the clan's mastermind.

So, she would become my "bad guy," and the chase was on. The rest would just have to fill itself in as I wrote. My research would have to be done from the comfort of my modern office, visiting various websites.

When author Jeff Guinn agreed to take a break from writing about cults and the exploits of Bonnie and Clyde and write a western trilogy, he exercised the same research techniques he'd used with his nonfiction. He visited locales he would be describing, read books about the time and place where his story would be set. If, in one of his westerns, he describes a craggy butte off in the distance, you can bet it is there. He is a meticulous researcher, and I greatly admire him for it.

Years earlier when I visited Benjamin Capps, another celebrated western author, to interview him for a profile, I saw that he had topographical maps pinned to his office walls to better detail the fictional cattle drive he was writing about.

But I had only ninety days.

Online, I found the make of weapons my characters would use, the breed of horse they were most likely to ride, and descriptions of the little towns they would visit. Guinn generously shared his list of what things (food, lodging, a shot of whiskey, and livery food for their mounts) had cost back then.

Though aware that western fiction was viewed by the academic elites as no high form of writing, I was determined to produce as good a book as possible in the time allotted.

Had I known more about what I was doing, I would have compiled a detailed outline to follow before beginning the first chapter. Instead, I winged it with a fuzzy plan that would provide my story of determined revenge a satisfactory beginning and end. I had a pretty good idea of where I was going, but there were days when I wasn't sure how to get there. I let imagination do its dance.

Minor characters occasionally asserted themselves and stepped forward to take the lead. My villain became increasingly mean-spirited. When they did, I made sure they spoke in an Old West vernacular that rang true but avoided an overabundance of "ain'ts" and labored bad grammar. No "purty" for "pretty," and no double negatives. I respected my characters too much to do that to them.

And in return they took over the story, doing and saying things for which I'd never planned.

The end results would be familiar to western readers. Good triumphed over evil. There was redemption and violence and even a hint of a love story (but no sex) involved before all was said and done. I hadn't even found it difficult to avoid the cursing as I wrote the dialogue.

By the time the three-month race ended, I had thoroughly enjoyed myself. I waited for a response and was thrilled the day my agent called to say the novel had been accepted. "You are now officially a novelist," he said. Who would have thought?

In competition with a field of highbrow literary fiction, *Comanche Trail* was ultimately named a finalist in the annual Texas Institute of Letters' Best First Novel category. No other original paperback made the cut. It later received the same recognition from the Western Fictioneers Peacemaker Awards judges.

It won neither, but I was pleased. For the first time in my writing career, I had been free of sticking to the facts, making sure every quote used was accurate, and agonizing over real people's reaction to their portrayals. Occasionally when feeling whimsical, I even gave the names of family and friends to some of my characters.

As of this writing, I've had six western novels published and would like to think I'm not yet done. My readers, I know, aren't Ivy League professors. And on our best days, Ralph Compton and I will never lure the harried housewife from her bodice-ripping romances and spy thrillers.

But don't forget that award-winning mystery writer Elmore Leonard, the undisputed king of dialogue, began his career writing one western after another.

I'll not waste your time with a lengthy diatribe on the differences in writing fiction and nonfiction. They're obvious. And, on at least one level, much the same. Lest I harp, let me mention once again that all writing is storytelling.

As a relative newcomer, my advice to anyone wishing to write fiction is short and simple. After all, I stumbled onto it.

I do know that if I had been dead set on writing the next *Grapes of Wrath* or *Gone with the Wind*, I'd have wasted a lot of time, energy, and paper. Same if I'd wanted to challenge the authors of best-selling political pot boilers and war stories.

My venture into fiction has been a welcome learning experience, begun with a subject that I found interesting and enjoyable. So, I suggest you pick wisely as you plan your fiction debut.

And please don't allow yourself to be fooled into the notion that writing a novel demands far greater vocabulary and elite skill than does a well-crafted book of nonfiction.

I recall once being asked by an academic organization if I would help judge entries in their annual novel writing competition. The task required me to review almost forty entries. And, in doing so, I soon came up with my personal definition of the so-called literary novel. It is woefully overwritten and lacks much plot. Many of the entrants must have worn out their thesaurus, searching out obscure, multisyllable words to use. I felt they were pruning, not writing.

No doubt, they would view my approach to authorship with similar disdain. But I'll match reviews and sales figures with most of them any day. And I would politely remind them that the vast majority of book buyers and library visitors read for pleasure, not an English lesson.

As a reader (mostly of mysteries by the likes of Michael Connally, Jonathan Kellerman, Thomas H. Cook, etc.), I am constantly aware of the pace of the book. To me, good fiction can be told at various speeds so long as it moves the story along and holds the readers' interest. A good whodunit may exceed the speed limit on every page while the buildup of a psychological thriller can flow slowly but steadily.

It is the writer's sworn duty to determine how best to handle a chase scene vs. a moment when the protagonist is pondering whatever impossible situation he finds himself in; when to ease up or floorboard it.

Pace, then, is one of the most vital ingredients at your disposal. Use it wisely. Even read a scene or two aloud now and then.

For several reasons, I wish that call from Tom Colgan had come sooner rather than later in my writing career. Had it, I might have spent more time in the world of make-believe. Riding Ralph Compton's coattails has been an enlightening learning experience. I think I'm now a better writer for having agreed to give fiction a try. In the process of novel writing, I felt I improved measurably with each book, learned new, subtle techniques I'd not known were available to me.

Before moving on, let's briefly revisit that friend of ours who is hard at work on the Great American Novel. You know him: he'll talk your ear off about it on the phone and after inviting you to lunch, will let gravy congeal on your chicken fried steak while he once again details his twisting plot and each of the new and fascinating characters he's come up with. Eventually, he'll get around to telling you that he's finally gotten the first few chapters written and wonders if you would mind reading them and giving him your thoughts. (All he really wants is your praise for the whiz-bang job he's doing. No constructive criticism is necessary.)

It's a trap you would be wise to avoid.

Never mind that you might be fighting a deadline of your own or simply don't have the slightest interest in the science fiction-fantasy-horror epic he's described to near death.

So, I've come up with this friendship-saving response: I suggest he stop talking about it and complete his masterpiece—edit it, rewrite it, and get it in the best shape possible. Then, and only then, will I read it and offer judgment. It's a safe out since, most likely, he'll never finish his ambitious undertaking.

Which is not to say the critique of a fellow writer isn't of value.

For years, Jeff Guinn and I have had a "reader" arrangement that has benefitted us both. I have read, chapter by chapter, his works on cult leader Jim Jones, the outlaw escapades of Bonnie and Clyde, and his excellent western trilogy while they were in progress. Jeff, a veteran talent, isn't one who needs idle praise. He wants another pair of eyes to look out for small faults in grammar, a chapter that might better work if it was pared down a bit, occasional spelling or punctuation mistakes, or a phrase that could be improved.

Sometimes he agrees with my assessments, sometimes he dismisses them with no harm done. All in all, though, I like to think in some small ways, I've helped get him out of a ditch or two over the years.

Certainly, he's helped me as he returns the favor by taking time to critique my works-in-progress.

The only time I ever worried he might be less than pleased with me came on a night in New York when *Go Down Together*, his excellent book on Bonnie and Clyde, was a finalist for the Edgar Award. I had been asked to serve as the presenter and privately hoped to hand him the statuette.

There I stood at the podium, award in one hand and the name of the winner in another. To my disappointment, the name wasn't Jeff's.

Later, he would say, "Man, you were standing there with the Edgar in your hand. I was sitting twenty feet away. There was a backdoor just off to your right. We could have made a clean getaway." He got over it.

Another frequent request an author can anticipate is for the "blurb," that quick sentence that winds up on the book cover promising the reader all manner of great things inside. Some publishers favor borrowing a favorable line lifted from a review. Others prefer something directly from another writer, the more well-known the better.

Though hardly a household name, I've done a number of blurbs over the years, mostly for writers who are friends or to whom I owe a favor. Honestly, I might oversell now and then, but I won't make the reader false promises. If I don't particularly care for the book, I just don't submit a blurb, claiming limited time or poor health.

I mean, who's going to welcome a note saying, "This one's a piece of . . . "?

Frankly, I view the time-honored blurb as little more than a quick massage of the author's ego. When the paperback edition of *Scream at the Sky* was published, its cover carried a line lifted from a *Philadelphia Inquirer* review suggesting, "Only Truman Capote's *In Cold Blood* may match what Stowers accomplishes here." Talk about over the top. But, hey, I loved it. My chest expanded considerably, and I wasted no time showing it around. Even read it aloud to the family.

Yet I can offer no evidence whatsoever that it sent sales skyrocketing.

Truth is, those of us who occasionally seek a kind blurb are not that far removed from the friend wanting you to read (and praise) his novel-in-progress. We all crave a kind word now and then.

Work for Hire

————

A LUCRATIVE GENRE can be the corporate history. Rarely does a day go by without someone wanting a book done on their business, be it the bank celebrating its fiftieth anniversary or the amazing success story of a fast-food chain. Their feats will rarely attract the attention of a traditional publishing house, so the CEO budgets a salary for a writer and the cost of producing the book.

The subject is seldom sexy, and the readers will most often be customers opening a new account, employees, and close family members. You'll be lucky if the subject matter causes you to wake early and stay up late writing. But bear in mind that it is important to those who hired you. And their pay scale is often better than the standard New York contract.

Be prepared for an education. Among the projects I've taken on were the rollicking adventures of an oil and gas wildcatter, a sporting goods business, the history of a professional football organization, a police department, and the ever-growing North Texas Municipal Water District, provider for millions of thirsty people. The only thing I knew on the latter subject was that when one turned on the faucet he could drink, bathe, fill the dog's water bowl, and water the lawn. Then, I learned a powerful lesson from Benjamin Franklin. "Only when the well runs dry do you realize the value of water."

I came to realize I was writing on an important subject.

To gather material for such an undertaking requires considerable research and countless interviews with experts who are more than happy to give you a step-by-step lesson on purification, conservation, annual budgets, and to explain the demands of opening a new reservoir. You may not be interested in the cost of laying a pipeline from here to yon, but the people you're writing for are and feel it is vital information.

It is, then, essential that you become familiar with what is important to the people you've contracted with. As one of my early manuscript readers looked over my accounts of various water providing projects the district had undertaken, he politely pointed out that I had failed to include the cost of each undertaking. Back to the drawing board I went.

So how do the company president and the writer connect? If you have some background in the field, he's likely to find you, either by simply asking around or reaching out to your agent. Since you'll not likely be the only candidate under consideration, be prepared for an interview and a grand tour of the operation they want you to write about. It wouldn't hurt to take a couple of your previously published works along as get-acquainted gifts.

Once everyone is in agreement that you're the writer for the job, negotiations are much like any other book-writing agreement. After learning specifically what they want the book to include, you determine how much time you'll require to provide a completed manuscript and what you'll need as compensation (including an estimate of expenses for travel that might be required). A lawyer for Widgets & Things will compose a contract or letter of agreement that will detail your fee and how it will be paid, what your deadline will be, whether someone in the company will want to read your manuscript in chapter-by-chapter increments or wait until the first draft of the book is completed. Be sure your agent or attorney reviews the agreement before you sign it. It is important to realize that while you're dealing with successful businesspeople and their attorneys, they most likely have had no previous experience working with the literary world.

As with ghostwriting, this is a line of work where one best leaves his ego at the door. Let's face it, chances are you will spend considerable time on a project that won't interest the masses. There will be no book signings and no reviews (except perhaps in the company newsletter) and no royalties once you have been fully paid.

I have friends who have made a comfortable living exclusively in this field. They have maintained a high level of professionalism and pride in authorship. So should you if you're considering signing up.

And, yes, as with any kind of assignment there is always the possibility of a land mine in wait.

Year ago, in what I fondly recall as my Desperation Days, the owner of a landmark eatery reached out. I'd never met him before but had heard he was difficult, even in dealing with his customers. Something of a real-life Soup Nazi, I'd been warned. Still, we met, we talked, and finally came to a financial agreement (which he immediately made clear he thought was excessive).

I was dreading my decision before having written a single word. Then good fortune struck. We had agreed I would receive half of my fee up front and the second installment when the book was completed to his satisfaction. Frankly, I had serious doubt he would be easily satisfied.

When his first check bounced, I found good cause for a legitimate escape.

Rubber Chicken Delight

BE AWARE that if you earn even the slightest degree of notoriety, you can expect invitations to come on down and talk about your latest book or share the secrets of writing for fun and profit. The guys at the Rotary Club will wonder if you can fit them into your schedule. Same with the Lions and Woodmen of the World who would love to have you. There's always a writers' group or book club looking for a guest speaker. Or the local high school hopes you can participate in career day or speak at its annual football banquet.

If not careful, you can make a second career of it. And more times than not the compensation for your time will be a healthy serving of rubber chicken and maybe a Certificate of Appreciation. I get a lot of coffee mugs since, it seems, most organizations seeking my wisdom are on their last financial legs.

It's a well-kept secret, but most do have a little money in the budget to pay a speaker but just don't want to turn loose of it unless asked. So, if you're bashful about holding your hand out (as most of us are), the best you can expect is to be asked to bring along a few of your books to sell after you've dazzled them for thirty minutes. If they don't ask, maybe you'll want to drop a hint.

Where, then, to draw the line? That depends on whether you enjoy public speaking. Too, bear in mind that your time is every bit as valuable as the guy who rotates your tires or cleans the gutters.

Be forewarned, the service organizations are sneaky critters. Their program chairperson will either (a) call with an invite that is so far in the future that you can't come up with a valid excuse or (b) plead that he's desperate for an emergency replacement since the chairperson of the local blood bank backed out at the last minute. Never mind that he or she is admitting to your face that you're second choice.

Then, there's the Chain Reaction Factor to bear in mind. At every noonday Rotary or Lions Club gathering, ol' Fred, a member of some affiliated club down the road, will have been introduced as one of the day's visitors. I can guarantee you that as soon as the meeting ends, he'll be shaking your hand, giving you his card, and inviting you to pay a visit to his organization. It can turn into a runaway train.

I can only hope you won't be as easy as I am.

Truth is, I enjoy speaking. I meet new people (who might even eventually read one of my books), get a few things off my chest, and receive an occasional slap on the back.

But, not always.

There was this librarians' organization I was asked to visit years ago. How difficult could that be? I'd praise the fine work they do, recall that wonderful childhood summer when I got my first library card, and be done with it.

I thought I was knocking them dead, until time came for questions.

I had emphasized the importance of getting youngsters into the habit of reading and pointed out that my young son's first positive experience had come when he read S. E. Hinton's best-selling juvenile novel, *The Outsiders*.

The blue-haired lady in the front row took the floor, hands on hips, and demanded to know if I had bothered to read any of Hinton's books? Was I aware they were about life in gangs and lawbreaking and all other manner of unsavory behavior? How, in heaven's name, could I permit my child to read such trash?

The day was lost, so I had my say.

Yes, I had read the young author's books and had been impressed, particularly after learning she'd written them as a teenager. Apparently, my adversary had skipped past the redemption and morals in her books. Or the acclaim Hinton had received during her career.

For my big finish, I made it clear that whatever it took to lure my son into the habit of reading was just fine with me, so long as it wasn't pornographic or encouraged the overthrow of the government.

The organization never asked me back.

I mentioned earlier being asked to present an award at the annual

Mystery Writers of America's dinner. Just speak for two to three minutes, then call the winner's name, I was instructed. Several of those who came before me seemed not to have gotten the memo. They droned on about their own fascinating careers and told lame jokes as the five hundred in attendance fidgeted in their seats. I felt particularly bad for the finalists waiting to learn if they had won.

I tossed away my carefully prepared notes as I was called to the podium. "I had a number of absolutely hilarious jokes and several heartwarming stories to tell," I explained, "but a friend at my table advised me to 'just tell us who won the damn Edgar.'" With that, I opened the envelope.

There was a thunder of applause before I could list the nominees and announce the winner. Some even got to their feet. Clearly, my most brief and best speech ever.

Aside from taking you away from your day job, I see little lasting damage to be done by low-income public speaking. If you're among those who can step to the mic and wing it, more power to you. Most of us are better served by sticking to the Boy Scouts' "Be Prepared" credo. Bear in mind, if your talk is boring, the listener has every right to assume your writing must be as well.

Some of my well-known friends have signed up with speakers bureaus and occasionally earn impressive fees. I'm not that good at it. But, yes, there have been times when I was well paid for my visits. I've done daylong seminars at writers' conferences, spoken to law enforcement groups and teachers' get-togethers, and even once was invited to be the guest speaker at a Mensa Society meeting. Talk about your fish out of water.

A final word of warning: unless you're asked specifically to speak about your political affiliation, don't go there—like Stephen King seems wont to these days. I recently read yet another of his angry rants against a former president who he denounced, on the record, as "a terrible president and terrible person." King has every right to his opinion, but were it not for the fact he's probably got a zillion dollars already stashed in the bank, I have to question the wisdom of such a public statement.

It's a matter of simple math. Let's assume half of the country's book readers are Democrats and the other half Republicans. Those of us desperate to scare up every paying customer possible can't afford to intentionally alienate 50 percent of the market. Vote as you please; even scream at the TV when the news is on, but consider keeping your opinions to yourself when you're standing at a podium.

I solved the problem years ago. If the Young Republicans call, I tell them I'm a Blue Dog Democrat. If it's a Democrat function inviting, I thank them kindly and say I'm a dyed-in-the-wool Republican. Hey, if its politics, everyone fudges the truth anyway, right?

Basketball legend Michael Jordan, spokesperson for athletic shoes bearing his name, has figured it out. "Republicans and Democrats both buy shoes," he observed. The same can be said for book purchasers.

My only real worthwhile advice, however, is to not overdo the rubber chicken. It's heartburn waiting to happen.

Promoting One's Wares

———

THIS WILL BE SHORT AND SWEET inasmuch as it is an aspect of the business that gives me headaches. I don't enjoy promoting myself, have generally failed miserably when I've tried, and simply never viewed the exercise as part of my job description. Whatever happened to the publicity department?

I used to join in at those weekend book signings where invariably there would be this well-dressed lady there to promote and sell her latest romance paperback. She'd come rattling up to the front of the bookstore and start unloading all manner of show-and-tell items. Since the store owner had either forgotten or just didn't want to go to the expense, she would arrive with a life-size poster of her book cover to strategically place on a nearby easel. She'd have plenty of giveaway novelties like keychains, bookmarks, pencils, business cards, and those old standards, the refrigerator magnets. Sometimes she would even bring and play a video of some interview she had done for a local cable TV show.

And, once all was said and done and she had sold maybe a half dozen books, she loaded everything up and headed for the next stop. She seemed happy, so why shouldn't I be for her?

It is called self-promotion, and it isn't my thing. Oh, I've done enough book signings to reach from here to Abilene, in places ranging from a new car showroom to a store that sold kitchen ware. I've arrived (on time) at places where they had forgotten I was coming, had times when the only question I was asked during a two-hour stay involved directions to the restroom, and more than once arrived to find that nary a one of my books was available.

A guy can take just so much.

In today's shrinking publishing environment, the author can expect to be called on to do much of whatever promotion his or her book will receive. Unless you're on the bestseller list already, don't expect coast-to-coast publicity junkets; forget the three-minute spot on the morning network shows or those full-page ads in the trades and big city papers.

Today, with the advent of social media, part of the new writer's contract agreement with his publisher is that he will even set up his own account so he (not the publisher) can alert the electronic millions of his pub date, public appearance, and pass along a few kind words written by a reviewer.

More and more, authors are hiring their own publicists.

To demonstrate my complete lack of understanding of what makes the business world turn, I must point out that I've never understood the rule of thumb whereby a publisher will pour every dime of its limited promotional budget into backing a book or author that will fly high alone while virtually ignoring the new talent peeking in the door. How does new talent get its place at the table when the bean counters doom it before it has a chance? Just asking.

And, since we're on the subject, I must admit that it escapes me why an author will go to the expense of purchasing all those promotional trinkets in an effort to sell a book for which the advance was small and sale forecasts far from celestial. I can only assume they get a kick out of doing that sort of thing. Me, not so much.

Yes, I do think a writer has a certain obligation to promote his work. And today's reality is that if you don't, no one will. So, where to start?

I've kept it simple. I continue to accept invitations to speak, thinking I just might spark someone's interest enough to buy a book. If a member of the media asks for an interview, I'm flattered and take a seat. When I'm in the neighborhood, I drop into a bookstore just to say hello and thanks to the book buyer. It's a subtle, word-of-mouth approach that I'm comfortable with.

And, I think, every bit as effective as refrigerator magnets.

And Finally . . .

———

IF YOU'VE STAYED with me this far, you have no doubt noticed that there's been no mention of online journalism, blogs, podcasts, Facebook, texting, reading from a handheld tablet, or doing interviews on Zoom.

I'm old school, happy as a lark when I can get my computer and printer to work. I still miss my rotary dial phone and feel not the slightest need to apologize for the fact I read only what I can hold in my hand and neatly stack by the bedside. I have a small collection of my audiobooks but have yet to listen to one, though I'm sure their readers are quite talented. *Within These Walls*, read by Tom Pile, was even an AudioBook Listener Award finalist recently.

If you want high tech blather, leave me out of it and visit your nearest IT department or talk to my grandkids.

Things are changing so fast these days that it is too late for me to try and keep up. My wife, only half in jest, suggests I should have plied my trade back in the old pulp days when everyone used manual typewriters and earned a penny a word.

If you're interested in learning about self-publishing, I know a guy who knows a guy.

That said, some of my cracker-barrel philosophy and writing suggestions may be as outdated as running boards by the time you read them. I hope not.

Author's Bibliography

True Crime

Careless Whispers (Taylor, 1986; Pocket Books, 1987;
St. Martin's Press softcover, 2001; St. Martin's True Crime Classics, 2006)

Innocence Lost (Pocket Books, 1990; Pocket Books softcover, 1991;
St. Martin's Press, 2004)

Open Secrets (Pocket Books, 1994; Pocket Books softcover, 1995;
St. Martin's softcover, 2002; St. Martin's True Crime Classics, 2008)

To the Last Breath (St. Martin's, 1998; St. Martin's softcover, 1999;
St. Martin's True Crime Classics, 2002; Thorndike (large print), 2002)

Sins of the Son (Hyperion, 1995; St. Martin's softcover, 2000)

Please...Don't Kill Me, with Bill Dear (Houghton Mifflin, 1989)
Ballentine softcover, 1990)

Scream at the Sky (St. Martin's, 2003; St. Martin's softcover, 2004;
Thorndike (large print), 2003)

FBI Undercover, with Larry Wansley (Pocket Books softcover, 1989)

Within These Walls, with Rev. Carroll Pickett (St. Martin's, 2002)

Death in a Texas Desert (Republic of Texas Press, 2003)

The Girl in the Grave (Stephen F. Austin Press, 2014)

Sports

The Randy Matson Story (Tafnews Press, 1971)

Spirit (Berkley softcover, 1973)

Journey to Triumph (Taylor, 1982)

Cowboys Chronicles (Eakin Press, 1984)

The Unsinkable Titanic Thompson (Eakin Press, 1982;
Paperjacks softcover, 1988; Palmer Magic softcover, 1992)

Reaching Higher, with Billy Olson (Word Books, 1984)

Friday Night Heroes (Eakin Press, 1983)

Marcus, with Marcus Allen (St. Martin's, 1997; St. Martin's softcover, 1998;
Transaction Publishers (large print), 2000)

Cotton Bowl Classics: The First 50 Years (Taylor, 1986)

Dallas Cowboys, 1960–1985 (Taylor, 1984)

Champions, with Wilbur Evans (Strode, 1978)

A Passion for Victory, with Jack Harris (Taylor Fine Books, 1990)

Dallas Cowboys Bluebook III, with Steve Perkins and Greg Aiello
(Taylor, 1982)

Dallas Cowboys Bluebook IV, with Greg Aiello (Taylor, 1983)

Dallas Cowboys Bluebook IX, with Jarrett Bell (Taylor, 1988)

Where Dreams Die Hard (Da Capo Press, 2005)

Oh, Brother How They Played the Game (State House Press, 2007)

Texas Football Legends (TCU Press, 2008)

Staubach: Portrait of the Brightest Star (Triumph Books, 2008)

General

Where the Rainbows Wait, with Trent Jones (Playboy Press, 1978)

Terlingua Teacher, with Trent Jones (Eakin Press, 1982;
Iron Mountain Press, 2005)

Happy Trails, with Roy Rogers and Dale Evans (Word Books, 1979;
Guidepost Books, 1979; Key-Word Books softcover, 1981;
Bantam softcover, 1981)

Partners in Blue (Taylor Fine Books, 1983)

I'll Take the Rest of the World (privately published, 2006)

Doc, with H. B. Hughes (Taylor Fine Books, 1976)

Don't Tell Me It's Impossible until I've Already Done It, with Pam Lontos
(William Morrow, 1986; Jove softcover, 1987)

Doc Howard's Boy (privately published chapbook, 2000)

101 Essential Texas Books, with Glenn Dromgoole (Abilene Christian
University Press, 2014)

On Texas Backroads (Texas Star Trading, 2019)

Tough Streets, Rough Skies and Sunday Sidelines, with Larry Wansley
(TCU Press, 2024)

Juvenile/Children's Books

Real Winning (Word Books, 1986)

The Overcomers (Word Books, 1978)

A Hero Named George (Community Justice Foundation, 1991)

Hard Lessons (Community Justice Foundation, 1994)

Strength of the Heart, with Marcus Allen (Andrew McMeel, 2000)

Fiction

Comanche Trail (Signet, 2014)

Phantom Hill (Signet, 2016; Wheeler (large print), 2016)

Reunion in Hell (Berkley, 2020)

Return to Gila Bend (Berkley, 2020)

Dalton's Justice (Berkley, 2021)

Seven Roads to Revenge (Berkley, 2021; Gale (large print), 2022)

About the Author

Carlton Stowers is a member of the Texas Literary Hall of Fame and the Texas Institute of Letters. The Dallas Press Club selected him as a Legend of North Texas Journalism. He's a member of the Big Country Athletic Hall of Fame and recipient of the A. C. Greene Award for Lifetime Achievement.